Florida

Bed & Breakfast
Cookbook

Recipes from the

Warmth and Hospitality

of Florida B&Bs,

Beach Resorts,

& Country Inns

By Becky LeJeune

9   8   7   6   5   4   3   2

ISBN 978-1-889593-22-7
PUBLISHED BY:
3D Press
a Big Earth Publishing company
1637 Pearl Street, Suite 201
Boulder, CO 80302

800-258-5830 (order toll free)
303-443-9687 (fax)
www.bigearthpublishing.com

FRONT COVER PHOTO: Casa De Rosa B&B
BACK COVER PHOTOS top: Adora Inn; middle: Carriage Way B&B; bottom left: Our House of St. Augustine B&B: bottom right: Harrington House Beachfront B&B
COVER AND TEXT DESIGN: Rebecca Finkel
EDITING: Becky LeJeune
PRINTED IN China by Imago

The Bed & Breakfast Cookbook Series was originated by Carol Faino & Doreen Hazledine of Peppermint Press in Denver, Colorado in 1996.

DISCLAIMER AND LIMITS OF LIABILITY

Florida

Florida, nick-named the Sunshine State for its subtropical climate and typically sunny weather, was claimed for Spain in 1513 by explorer Ponce de León. He may not have been the first Spaniard to discover the land, though, as there were reports that León actually encountered natives already speaking Spanish. Regardless, León landed on April 2, 1513 and dubbed the land La Florida in honor of Pascua Florida, or Flowery Easter. Archaeologists have determined that Florida was inhabited for thousands of years prior to Spain's discovery.

England and Spain traded the state back and forth until the United States finally gained control in 1819. On March 3, 1845, Florida became the 27th official state to join the United States of America. On January 10, 1861, however, the state ceded from the union in anticipation of the outbreak of war. Just days later, Florida would become the founding member of the Confederacy.

Today, Florida is the fourth largest state by population and estimates say that by 2011, it will beat out New York for the third place position. It wasn't until the mid-twentieth century, though, that Florida's population began booming. The invention of air-conditioning, the climate, and the affordable cost of living all caused a sharp increase in the number of residents. Cape Canaveral and NASA brought a sizeable aerospace industry to the state and there's also been a recent boom in the medical and bio-tech industries. Citrus fruit, sugarcane, and strawberries are a few of the state's biggest crops and enough seafood is harvested from the coastal waters to make Florida one of the top five states in the industry.

With its hundreds of miles of beaches, and of course the Disney theme parks, tourism makes up much of the economy – the Disney World Resort alone attracts more visitors than any other amusement park in the States.

STATE SYMBOLS

STATE ANIMAL:
Florida Panther

STATE BEVERAGE:
Orange Juice

STATE BIRD: Mockingbird

STATE FLOWER:
Orange Blossom

STATE TREE:
Sabal Palmetto Palm

STATE MARINE MAMMAL:
Manatee

STATE REPTILE:
American Alligator

STATE GEM:
Moonstone

STATE PIE: Key Lime Pie

STATE FRUIT: Orange

STATE NICKNAME:
The Sunshine State

STATE MOTTO: In God we trust

STATE SONG: Swanee River

FAMOUS FLORIDIANS

Bob Vila
Emmitt Smith
Faye Dunaway
Carl Hiaasen
Zora Neale Hurston
Lauren Hutton
Jim Morrison
Charles & John Ringling
Sidney Poitier
Janet Reno

GEOGRAPHICAL FEATURES OF NOTE

- Britton Hill is the highest point in the state. At just 345 feet, it is also the lowest high point in all of the United States.

- Everglades and Everglades National Park are part of a vast wetland system that encompasses Southern Florida and is home to a wide variety of rare and endangered species.

- The only extensive coral reefs in the continental U.S. can be found off the Atlantic coast of Florida. This the third largest reef system in the world

FUN FACTS ABOUT FLORIDA

- No part of the state is more than 75 miles from Atlantic or Gulf waters.

- In 1890, Key West was the most populous city in Florida.

- More hurricanes have made landfall in Florida that anywhere else in the world.

- The Benwood, on French Reef in the Florida Keys, is known as one of the most dived shipwrecks in the world.

- Miami Beach pharmacist Benjamin Green invented the first sunscreen in 1944.

- Gatorade was invented by University of Florida medical researchers in 1965.

Contents

Breads & Muffins

Breads
& Muffins

*Good bread is the most fundamentally
satisfying of all foods; and good bread
with fresh butter, the greatest of feasts.*

—JAMES BEARD

INN SHEPARD'S PARK B&B

Inn Shepard's Park was built in 1924 from the reclaimed lumber of the old Danforth Hotel that once stood on the St. Lucie River. Today, this Key West-style home has four guest rooms with assorted unique themes. Décor includes wicker accents and four-poster and iron beds outfitted with cozy quilts and comforters. Guests can take advantage of the inn's many common areas as well. The sunroom is great for an afternoon of reading, the parlor is perfect for getting to know fellow travelers, the wrap-around porch is a wonderful place to enjoy a cold glass of iced tea, and the hammocks out back are just the place to enjoy a quiet afternoon nap.

"After a long week traveling for business, a stay [at the Inn Shepard's Park] was just what the doctor ordered. It's located in a beautiful, quiet area near the waterfront. The hot tub and comfy bed made all the difference in the world… I could easily have stayed a week. Looking forward to coming back again!" —GUEST

INNKEEPER:	Marilyn Miller
ADDRESS:	601 SW Ocean Blvd., Stuart, Florida 34994
TELEPHONE:	(772) 781-4244
E-MAIL:	marilyn@innshepard.com
WEBSITE:	www.innshepard.com
ROOMS:	4 Rooms; Private & shared baths
CHILDREN:	Children age 12 and older welcome
PETS:	Dogs welcome; Resident pets

Pineapple Bread

Makes 6 Servings

½ cup butter
1 cup sugar
4 eggs, beaten
20 ounces crushed pineapple, drained
5 pieces good white bread, cubed

Preheat oven to 350°F. In a medium bowl, cream together the butter and sugar; add the eggs and mix to combine. Using a spoon or rubber spatula, fold in the pineapple and the cubed bread. Pour the mixture into a greased 9x9-inch baking dish and bake 55 minutes, until the top is browned. Serve hot or cold.

The average pineapple typically weighs between four and nine pounds, but they have been known to grow as large as twenty pounds.

Victorian House B&B

Conveniently located in the heart of St. Augustine, the oldest city in the U.S., is this charming Victorian inn. Originally built in 1895, the home was lovingly restored in 1983. The entire inn, including its five guest rooms, and five suites, has been carefully outfitted with tasteful and unique décor, antiques, and heirlooms. The inn sits between two of the oldest streets, in a quiet residential area that is literally just steps from the town plaza. The inn's emphasis on comfort, elegance, and hospitality has earned it much praise—they've been called "The Inn With the Most Privacy," one of the "Top 100 Gold Inns" in the U.S. and were included in *Florida Monthly Magazine's* list of "Florida's Fabulous Bed and Breakfast Inns."

All guests are treated to a hearty homemade breakfast and complimentary beverages, including Amaretto, and fresh baked cookies and fudge every day. Guests looking for an extra-special something should check out the Victorian House's list of special packages. Packages feature items like romantic carriage rides, champagne and truffles, dinner for two at a local restaurant, flowers, or even lunch picnic basket. The inn also specializes in small weddings and anniversaries.

INNKEEPERS:	Marc & Jackie Rude
ADDRESS:	11 Cadiz Street, St. Augustine, FL 32084
TELEPHONE:	(904) 824-5214; (877) 703-0432
E-MAIL:	victorianhouse@bellsouth.net
WEBSITE:	www.victorianhousebnb.com
ROOMS:	5 Rooms; 5 Suites; Private baths
CHILDREN:	Children age 8 and older welcome
PETS:	Not allowed; Resident pet

Strawberry Walnut Bread

Makes 2 Loaves

*"Unusual flavor combination. Cardamom is a popular spice
used in Scandinavian countries."*

—INNKEEPER, *Victorian House Bed & Breakfast*

2 cups finely chopped walnuts
3 cups flour
1 teaspoon baking soda
1½ teaspoon cinnamon
1 teaspoon ground cardamom,
    may substitute additional cinnamon
½ teaspoon salt
¼ teaspoon nutmeg
1 tablespoon finely shredded orange peel
4 beaten eggs
2 cups sugar
1½ cups mashed strawberries
    (about 3 cups whole berries)
1 cup mashed banana
1 cup vegetable oil

Preheat oven to 350°F and spray two 9-inch loaf pans with non-stick cooking spray. Sprinkle about ½ cup of the nuts into the bottom of each pan. In a large bowl, combine the flour, baking soda, cinnamon, cardamom, salt, nutmeg, and orange peel. In a separate bowl, combine the eggs, sugar, strawberries, banana, and oil. Add the wet mixture to the dry ingredients and stir until just moistened. Fold in the remaining nuts and divide the batter evenly between the two loaf pans. Bake 1 hour, or until a toothpick inserted in the center comes away clean. Allow the bread to cool in the pans for 10 minutes before removing to wire racks. Cool completely before wrapping in plastic wrap to store.

Lemon Poppyseed Bread

Makes 4 Small Loaves

"Sweet and light!"

—INNKEEPER, *Victorian House Bed & Breakfast*

1 (10.25 ounce) package dry lemon cake mix
1 (3.4 ounce) small package dry lemon instant pudding
3 large eggs
1 tablespoon poppy seeds
1 cup water
½ cup canola oil

Preheat oven to 325°F. Place all of the ingredients in a large bowl and whisk together to mix. Line the bottoms of four small loaf pans with parchment or wax paper, then spray non-stick cooking spray onto the sides. Divide the batter evenly between the pans. Place the pans on the center rack and bake 40-50 minutes, or until a toothpick inserted in the center comes away clean.

The poppy seed has been cultivated for over 3,000 years. In addition to being used to add flavor to cakes and breads, you can also use them as a spice in pie crust, cookies, salad dressings, and in sauces for meats.

Zucchini Bread

Makes 2 Loaves

*"Some guests may need convincing to try this recipe.
When my husband hears doubters in a group, he always mentions
carrot cake and how yummy it is. The guests understand the
correlation and quickly succumb!"*
—INNKEEPER, *Victorian House Bed & Breakfast*

3¼ cups flour
1½ teaspoons salt
1 teaspoon nutmeg
2 teaspoons baking soda
1 teaspoon cinnamon
3 cups sugar
1 cup vegetable oil
4 eggs, lightly beaten
$\frac{1}{3}$ cup water
2 cups grated zucchini
1 teaspoon lemon juice
1 cup chopped walnuts

Preheat oven to 350°F and spray two 9-inch loaf pans with non-
stick cooking spray. In a large bowl, sift together the flour, salt,
nutmeg, baking soda, cinnamon, and sugar. In a separate bowl,
combine the vegetable oil, eggs, water, grated zucchini, and lemon
juice. Pour the wet mixture into the dry mixture and stir to fully
incorporate. Fold in the chopped nuts and divide the batter evenly
between the two loaf pans. Bake 1 hour, or until a toothpick
inserted in the center comes away clean.

CAMELLIA ROSE INN

Just a short stroll from historic downtown Gainesville, home of the University of Florida, sits the charming Camellia Rose Inn. The Inn is perfectly located away from the high traffic tourist areas, but a short drive from the most popular destinations. Here you can truly get away from it all, but still have access to anything you might be looking for. Stay the weekend and enjoy a Gators game, relax and spend some time with that special someone, or take a day trip to town. When you return in the evening, you'll find home-made goodies waiting for you before you retire for the evening.

Complimentary beverages and snacks are provided at the Camellia Rose Inn's daily happy hour, and are a great way to unwind. In the morning, a full three-course breakfast is just the way to start your day. Selections such as cream cheese scrambled eggs, seasonal fruit, biscuits and gravy, and cheesy garlic grits are sure to tide you over for most of the day!

INNKEEPERS: Pat & Tom McCants

ADDRESS: 205 SE 7th Street, Gainesville, Florida 32601

TELEPHONE: (352) 395-7673

E-MAIL: info@camelliaroseinn.com

WEBSITE: www.camelliaroseinn.com

ROOMS: 6 Rooms; 1 Cottage; Private baths

CHILDREN: Welcome

PETS: Welcome; Call ahead; Resident pets

Zucchini Nut Bread

Makes 2 Loaves

3 cups all-purpose flour
1½ teaspoons ground cinnamon
1 teaspoon baking soda
½ teaspoon baking powder
½ teaspoon salt
3 eggs
2 cups sugar
1 cup canola oil
1 tablespoon vanilla extract
2 cups shredded zucchini
½ cup chopped walnuts or pecans

Preheat oven to 350°F. In a large bowl, combine the flour, cinnamon, baking soda, baking powder, and salt. In a separate bowl, beat together the eggs, sugar, oil, and vanilla. Add the wet mixture to the dry ingredients and stir until just combined. Fold in the zucchini and nuts. Grease and flour two 8x4x2-inch loaf pans. Pour the mixture evenly into the pans and bake 55-60 minutes, or until loaves are browned and a toothpick inserted in the center comes away clean.

Cool 10 minutes and remove to a wire rack. Wrap in foil to store.

Tips and Variations

This bread will refrigerate for up to a week and freezes very well.

Camellia Rose Inn Banana Bread

Makes 1 Loaf

2 eggs
2 very ripe bananas, mashed
½ cup canola oil
¼ cup plus 1 tablespoon buttermilk
1 teaspoon vanilla extract
1¾ cups all-purpose flour
1½ cups sugar
1 teaspoon baking soda
½ teaspoon salt
1 cup chopped pecans (optional)

Preheat oven to 350°F and lightly grease an 8½ x 4¼–inch loaf pan.
Place the eggs, mashed bananas, canola oil, buttermilk, and vanilla
in a medium mixing bowl and beat with an electric mixer until
creamy and well blended. In a separate bowl, sift together the flour,
sugar, baking soda, and salt; add to the wet mixture and beat at low
speed until just incorporated. Stir in pecans. Bake for 60 minutes, or
until a toothpick inserted in the center comes away clean. Remove
from oven and allow to cool on a wire rack for 20 minutes. Run
a knife along the edges of the pan to loosen the bread and remove
from loaf pan; continue cooling on rack.

Tips and Variations

Tip: Bake the bread, covered, for the first 20 minutes
to prevent too much browning.

QUICK BREADS, like banana and zucchini, were most likely developed inthe late 18th century when pearlash was discovered. Pearlash is the result of baking potassium carbonate to remove impurities. This method was patented by Samuel Hopkins in 1790. Pearlash produces carbon dioxide in dough causing it to rise — the same reason we use baking powder today.

Zucchini, being fairly easy to grow and producing abundant fruit, was most likely experimented with early on since people would have been looking for as many ways as possible to use it. Bananas are another popular ingredient in quick breads because it's a quick and easy way to use up the over-ripe ones.

Harrington House
Beachfront
Bed & Breakfast

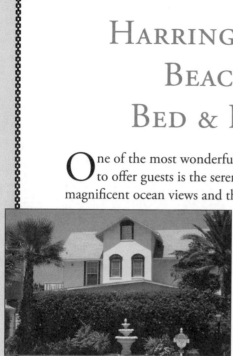

One of the most wonderful things that Harrington House has to offer guests is the serene and tranquil beach setting. The magnificent ocean views and the sounds of the waves are both calming and romantic. Each morning wake to the sun rising over the ocean and enjoy a full island breakfast, made from scratch and featuring a wide variety of ever changing options. In the evening, enjoy some of the homemade cookies or even a basket of fresh popcorn while you watch the sunset. Then, let the sounds of the ocean rock you to sleep. The intimate atmosphere is true rejuvenation for the soul.

*"Our stay at Harrington house was amazing; from the dolphin and pelican shows to the magical sunsets and star gazing from the pool. The staff is friendly and accommodating. The island is laid back and relaxing. The beach is quiet. Definitely one of the best places we've stayed." —*GUEST

INNKEEPERS: Patti & Mark Davis

ADDRESS: 5626 Gulf Drive, Holmes Beach, Florida 34217

TELEPHONE: (941) 778-5444; (888) 828-5566

E-MAIL: fbbi@harringtonhouse.com

WEBSITE: www.harringtonhouse.com

ROOMS: 20 Rooms; Private baths

CHILDREN: Children age 12 and older welcome

PETS: Not allowed

Buttermilk Banana Nut Bread

Makes 2 Loaves

*"This recipe originated from a woman named Iris Sachs.
Iris worked with us for several years before moving back to her
hometown of Copake Falls, New York. We have continued to use her
original recipe for the last 20 years that we have been in business."*
—INNKEEPER, *Harrington House Beachfront B&B*

1 cup melted butter
2 cups sugar
1 teaspoon vanilla extract
2 eggs
1 cup buttermilk
4 ripe bananas, mashed
1 teaspoon baking soda
1 teaspoon baking powder
Dash salt
2½ cups flour
Chopped walnuts or pecans, optional

Preheat oven to 350°F. Grease 2 9-inch loaf pan and line just the bottom with waxed paper. Using an electric mixer, combine the melted butter, sugar, vanilla extract, eggs, buttermilk, and bananas together in a large mixing bowl. In a separate bowl, sift together the baking soda, baking powder, salt, and the flour. Add the dry mixture to the wet mixture and mix well to combine. Using a rubber spatula or spoon, fold in the nuts if using. Divide the batter evenly between the loaf pans and bake 50-60 minutes, or until a toothpick inserted into the center of the bread comes away clean. Easy and delicious!

ALLISON HOUSE INN

A llison House Inn is a charming English-style b&b located in
the heart of Quincy's 36-block historic district. Throughout
the years, the inn has been voted the Most Historic Inn, the Best
Breakfast in the Southeast, and the Most Affordable Luxury Bed
& Breakfast. Owners Stuart and Eileen are dedicated to providing
guests with a vacation they will always remember. Their attention

to every detail is apparent from
the lavender scented pillow-
cases to the homemade biscotti
and sherry available throughout the day.

Weekday guests are treated
to a daily European-style
breakfast that features a variety
of baked goods, juices, fresh fruit, and the inn's signature granola
and homemade marmalade. A full gourmet breakfast is served on
the weekends with selections ranging from stuffed French toast and
crêpes to baked eggs and quiches.

INNKEEPER: Stuart Johnson

ADDRESS: 215 North Madison Street, Quincy, Florida 32351

TELEPHONE: (850) 875-2511; (888) 904-2511

E-MAIL: innkeeper@tds.net

WEBSITE: www.allisonhouseinn.com

ROOMS: 6 Rooms; Private baths

CHILDREN: Welcome

PETS: Small dogs welcome

Camilla's Allison House Inn Banana Bread

Makes 2 Loaves

*"This is my mother's recipe and is very popular at the inn.
I bake small, individual loaves for the guests at breakfast."*

—INNKEEPER, *Allison House Inn*

½ cup shortening
1 cup sugar
2 eggs
2 cups flour
1 teaspoon baking soda
⅓ cup milk
1 teaspoon lemon juice
1 cup mashed bananas
½ cup walnuts, coarsely chopped (optional)

Preheat oven to 325°F. In a large bowl, blend together the shortening, sugar, and eggs. In a separate bowl, sift together the flour and baking soda. Add half of the flour mixture to the shortening mixture, blend in the milk, lemon, and banana before adding the remaining flour. Fold in the chopped walnuts.

Spray two 9-inch loaf pans with non-stick cooking spray and divide the dough evenly between the pans. Bake about 1 hour, or until the bread is golden brown and a toothpick inserted in the center comes out clean. Cool on wire racks before removing from pan.

ELIZABETH POINTE LODGE

 The Elizabeth Pointe Lodge on lovely Amelia Island is a luxurious and relaxing beach resort with everything you could want for the ultimate in pampered vacation experiences. The inn actually consists of three buildings, the 1890s Nantucket shingle-style main house, the adjacent Ocean House, and the Miller Cottage. The main house has twenty of the inn's guest rooms and is set up with a unique maritime theme; the Ocean House features West Indies style décor and houses four of the inn's larger guest suites. The Cottage is perfect for vacationing families and also houses a state-of-the-art corporate meeting facility.

The view from the inn is absolutely to die for. Elizabeth Pointe looks right out onto the water and the porches are the perfect spot to watch a sunset with that special someone. Breakfast is served each morning in the oceanfront sunroom and lemonade is served every day on the porch, or right out on the beach. The inn also has an evening wine and hors d'oeuvres service at 6pm. And, because the innkeepers definitely understand when guests don't want to leave, they can fix you up a light lunch or dinner, and even have dessert available all day long. So, whether you want to stay in and cuddle with your sweetheart all day, or ride a bike into town for some sight-seeing and shopping, Amelia Island's Elizabeth Pointe Lodge is the perfect vacation destination.

INNKEEPERS: David & Susan Caples

ADDRESS: 98 South Fletcher Avenue, Amelia Island, Florida 32034

TELEPHONE: (904) 277-4851; (800) 772-3359

E-MAIL: info@elizabethpointelodge.com

WEBSITE: www.elizabethpointelodge.com

ROOMS: 24 Rooms; 1 Cottage; Private baths

CHILDREN: Welcome

PETS: Not allowed

Miss Ona's Orange Juice Bread

Makes 1 Loaf

*"Miss Ona, a true Southern cook born and raised in
Fernandina Beach, developed this original recipe
using oranges from the trees in her own yard."*
—INNKEEPER, *Elizabeth Pointe Lodge*

½ cup sweet butter
1¼ cups sugar
2 large eggs
1½ cups unbleached white flour
1 teaspoon baking powder
¼ teaspoon salt
¼ cup orange juice
¼ cup milk
Zest of 1 lemon, grated,
    or ½ teaspoon lemon peel
Zest or 1 orange, grated,
    or ½ teaspoon orange peel

Icing:
1 tablespoon lemon juice
1 tablespoon orange juice
$\frac{1}{3}$ cup confectioners sugar

Preheat oven to 350°F and butter a 9-inch loaf pan. In a large bowl,
cream together the butter and the sugar. Beat the eggs and add to
the creamed mixture. In a medium bowl, sift together the flour,
baking powder, and salt. In a separate bowl, mix together the
orange juice and the milk. Add the liquids alternately with the
sifted dry ingredients to the creamed mixture, a little at a time,
beating well after each addition. Stir in the lemon and orange
zest. Line the bottom of the buttered loaf pan with waxed paper
and butter the waxed paper. Smooth the batter over the waxed
paper and bake 45 minutes, or until the bread springs back lightly
when touched. Remove the bread from the pan and allow to cool
15 minutes before removing the waxed paper. Drizzle with icing
before serving.

For the icing: Stir the lemon and orange juice into the sugar until
well combined.

Tips and Variations

This bread is especially good for breakfast or spread with thick butter and
served as an accompaniment with afternoon tea.

Sunrise Muffins

Makes 12 Regular Muffins, 24 Mini-Muffins, or 1 9-inch Loaf

"The Elizabeth Pointe Lodge has been serving this recipe for the past 17 years, first as mini muffins, and now as a sweet bread. We serve them on our breakfast buffet and as a side with our light fare lunch menu."
—INNKEEPER, *Elizabeth Pointe Lodge*

1 cup grated carrot
¼ cup shredded coconut
½ cup diced Granny Smith apples
¼ cup seedless raisins
¼ cup chopped pecans
1 cup whole wheat flour
1 teaspoon baking soda
¼ teaspoon salt
⅔ cup granulated sugar
½ teaspoon cinnamon
2 eggs, slightly beaten
½ cup vegetable oil
1 teaspoon vanilla extract

Preheat oven to 350°F and grease a mini-muffin tin with Crisco. In a large bowl, combine the carrots, coconut, apples, raisins, and pecans; set aside. In a large mixing bowl, combine the flour, baking soda, salt, sugar, and cinnamon. Make a hole in the center of the dry mixture and add the eggs, oil, and vanilla. Stir the wet ingredients into the dry ingredients until smooth. Fold in the fruit and nut mixture, stirring until well blended. Using a spoon, scoop the mixture into each muffin cup until ¾ full. Bake 10 minutes and test with a toothpick for doneness. Once the toothpick comes away clean, the muffins are ready to be pulled from the oven. Remove the muffins from their cups and place on a cooling rack.

Tips and Variations

To make this as a bread or regular sized muffins, grease a 9-inch loaf pan or 12 cup muffin tin and follow directions above. Cook time will need to be adjusted accordingly for regular sized-muffins or loaf (approximately 15-20 minutes for regular muffins and 45-60 minutes for bread).

The word MUFFIN most likely derived from the German muffen or small cake. Early versions of muffins were much less sweet than today's creations and lacked the variety of ingredients as well. They were also notorious for going stale rather quickly. In the 1950s several different companies both here and abroad began producing packaged muffin mixes and by the 1960s, coffee shops were beginning to appear. Both of these occurrences made the muffin more popular as they were now readily beginning to appear outside of home kitchens for the first time. The 70s and the 80s saw a decline in home cooking and an increase in the search for healthier food options as well as a boom in the gourmet coffee market. Today, you can hit any local coffee shop for a variety of these little cake concoctions.

KING'S MANOR B&B

This circa 1884 Victorian farmhouse in charming Oviedo, Florida sits nestled among historic oaks on two acres of land. Since it was built, the home has only passed through just four family's hands. George Hazeltine Browne, speaker of the House of Representatives in Florida in 1887, built the home and lived there

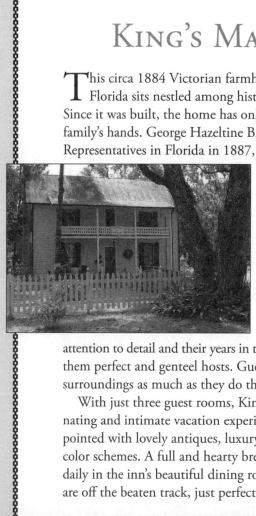

until 1890. The next family, the Kings, owned the home until 1970. The McCarley family came next, and they sold the home to current owners in 1992. Roberta and Paul McQueen have fully restored the home and even earned its place on the National Register of Historic Places. Their loving attention to detail and their years in the hospitality industry have made them perfect and genteel hosts. Guests love the quiet and peaceful surroundings as much as they do the elegant and stately home.

With just three guest rooms, King's Manor offers guests a rejuvenating and intimate vacation experience. Each room is uniquely appointed with lovely antiques, luxury bedding, and soft and soothing color schemes. A full and hearty breakfast of your choice is served daily in the inn's beautiful dining room. King's Manor and Oviedo are off the beaten track, just perfect for getting away from it all.

INNKEEPERS: Roberta & Paul McQueen
ADDRESS: 322 King Street, Oviedo, Florida 32765
TELEPHONE: (407) 365-4200
E-MAIL: kingsmanor@bellsouth.net
WEBSITE: www.kingsmanorbb.com
ROOMS: 3 Rooms; Private baths
CHILDREN: Cannot accommodate
PETS: Not allowed; Resident pet

Blueberry Muffin Tops

Makes 12 Muffins or 6 Tops

"These are the most popular muffins I make,
according to our long-stay guests."
—INNKEEPER, *King's Manor B&B*

¾ stick unsalted butter, melted
⅓ cup whole milk
1 large egg
1 large egg yolk
¾ teaspoon vanilla extract
1 – 1½ cups all-purpose flour
¾ cup sugar
1½ teaspoons baking powder
¾ teaspoon salt
1½ cups fresh blueberries

Topping:
3 tablespoons unsalted butter, cut into bits
½ cup all-purpose flour

Preheat oven to 375°F and spray a muffin pan with non-stick cooking spray. In a medium bowl, whisk together the melted butter and milk. Add the whole egg, egg yolk, and vanilla extract until and mix until well combined. In a separate bowl, whisk together the flour, sugar, baking powder, and salt. Add the milk mixture to the dry mixture and mix until just combined. Gently fold in the blueberries. Spoon the batter into greased muffin cups, filling them about ¾ of the way. In a small bowl, crumble together the flour and butter for the topping; crumble the topping mixture over each muffin. Bake 18-20 minutes, until the muffins are golden and a toothpick inserted in the center comes away clean. Cool in the pan for 15 minutes before carefully removing. Serve warm or at room temperature.

MAGNOLIA PLANTATION B&B INN

The Magnolia Plantation B&B Inn is a series of nine cottages that surrounds a main house. The main inn was built 1885 by lumberman Dudley Williams and his wife Melinza. The architectural style of the home is what's referred to as French Second Empire, characterized by the tall front tower and the mansard roof. This particular style is quite uncommon in this area.

The house is most commonly known as the Baird Mansion in honor of the family that lived there for almost seventy years. Emmett Baird owned and operated a sawmill and the Standard Crate Company. It was rumored that Baird discovered pirate's treasure at Fowlers Bluff in the late 1800s. It was said that he used this fortune to purchase Baird Mansion and that he stashed the remaining treasure somewhere in the house just before his death. Owners Joe & Cindy discovered no pirate treasure while renovating the home!

INNKEEPERS:	Joe & Cindy Montalto
ADDRESS:	309 SE 7th Street, Gainesville, Florida 32601
TELEPHONE:	(352) 375-6653; (800) 201-2379
E-MAIL:	info@magnoliabnb.com
WEBSITE:	www.magnoliabnb.com
ROOMS:	5 Rooms; 9 Cottages; Private baths
CHILDREN:	Welcome; Call ahead
PETS:	Welcome; Call ahead; Resident pets

Piña Colada Muffins

Makes 24 Muffins

1 (1 pound) box yellow or butter cake mix
1 teaspoon pure coconut extract
1 teaspoon pure rum extract
1 cup flaked coconut
1 cup chopped nuts
1 (8 ounce) can crushed pineapple, un-drained

Preheat oven to 350°F. Prepare the cake batter according to package directions. Add the extracts, coconut, nuts, and pineapple with juice and mix 1 minute – do not overmix. Grease the cups of a muffin tin and fill each about ¾ full. Bake 15-20 minutes, or until golden brown.

There are three places that claim to have invented the first Piña Colada sometime between the 1950s and the 1960s: The Caribe Hilton Hotel in Puerto Rico, a bar in Old San Juan, and the Barrachina restaurant in Puerto Rico, but *Travel* magazine first mentioned the drink in a December 1922 article.

PELICAN PATH B&B
BY THE SEA

Pelican Path is a relaxing oceanfront inn located in heavenly Jacksonville, Florida. The close proximity to the ocean is great for guests looking to lounge on the beach and soak in the sun. You can also take one of the inn's bikes and tour around the area. While you're there, you won't wan to miss Jacksonville's many attractions.

Jacksonville has a host of things to offer vacationers. You can rent beach stuff and have it delivered directly to you at Pelican Path. Call up Bananas Sailing Charters and book an eco-tour, an evening of sailing, or even a romantic dinner cruise. Visit the Jacksonville Zoo, tour the Kingsley Plantation, the oldest remaining plantation in all of Florida, and visit the Fort Caroline National Memorial. Enjoy some world-class golf and deep-sea or freshwater fishing. Whatever you're looking for, Jacksonville has it.

INNKEEPERS:	Joan & Tom Hubbard
ADDRESS:	11 North 19th Avenue, Jacksonville, Florida 32250
TELEPHONE:	(904) 249-1177; (888) 749-1177
E-MAIL:	ppbandb@aol.com
WEBSITE:	www.pelicanpath.com
ROOMS:	4 Rooms; Private baths
CHILDREN:	Cannot accommodate
PETS:	Not allowed

Pecan Pie Muffins

Makes 3 Dozen Mini-muffins

*"This wonderful recipe, given to me by my dental hygienist,
was almost discarded. Although they were delicious,
the muffins were impossible to get out of the pan. Tom suggested
that I add an additional egg to the original recipe to help hold them
together — it made all the difference. Now the recipe is perfect!"*

—INNKEEPER, *Pelican Path B&B by the Sea*

> 1 cup brown sugar
> ½ cup all-purpose flour
> 3 eggs
> ²⁄₃ cup melted butter
> 1 cup chopped pecans
> Pecan halves for topping

Preheat oven to 350°F. In a medium bowl, mix together the sugar, flour, eggs, melted butter, and chopped pecans; mix well to fully combine. Grease the cups of a mini-muffin tin and fill each cup ²⁄₃ full of batter. Place a pecan half on top of each muffin and bake 14 minutes.

To make a smaller batch (1½-2 dozen mini-muffins) use the following measurements: ²⁄₃ cup brown sugar, ⅓ cup flour, 2 eggs, ½ cup melted butter, and 2²⁄₃ cup chopped pecans. Follow baking directions as above.

GRADY HOUSE
BED & BREAKFAST

High Springs, Florida was established in the late 1800s as a railroad town. In 1917, the building that would become Grady House was built on the site of a former bakery and was originally a boarding house for the railroad's supervisors. The adjoining Skeet's Cottage was built in 1896. The home, actually called Easterlin House, earned it's nickname courtesy of it's once infamous resident, Juanita "Skeet" Easterlin. Easterlin was the first female mayor of High Springs.

In the mid-1950s Easterlin ran for re-election and promised to tighten local liquor laws. Just a year later, she was busted for running her very own moonshine ring!

Today, Grady House and the Skeet Cottage have been fully renovated to blend its historic past with the best of today's modern conveniences. Each of the inn's six guest rooms features period antiques and lush featherbeds with down pillows. Each room is slightly different and may have either a walk-in shower or claw-foot tub. The Skeet Cottage is perfect for larger parties or those seeking a bit more privacy. It has a full kitchen, family room, and parlor and can accommodate up to four guests. The inn is also known for it's magnificent gardens, which feature walking paths, a jasmine-covered gazebo, and a water garden complete with waterfall and koi pond.

INNKEEPERS: Paul & Lucie Regensdorf
ADDRESS: 420 NW 1st Avenue, High Springs, FL 32643
TELEPHONE: (386) 454-2206
E-MAIL: gradyhouse@gradyhouse.com
WEBSITE: www.gradyhouse.com
ROOMS: 2 Rooms; 3 Suites; 1 Cottage
CHILDREN: Children age 10 and older welcome
PETS: Not allowed; Resident pets

Sausage and Cheddar Cheese Muffins

Makes 10 Muffins

1 (1 pound) package ground pork sausage
3 cups all-purpose baking mix
1½ cups shredded cheddar cheese
1 (15½ ounce) jar salsa con queso
¾ cup water

Preheat oven to 375°F. In a large skillet over medium high heat, cook the sausage, stirring until it crumbles and is no longer pink. Drain and cool. Combine the sausage, baking mix, and shredded cheese in a large bowl. Add the salsa con queso and water and stir until the mixture is completely moistened. Lightly grease the cups of a 12-cup muffin tin. Spoon the batter into the cups, filling them to the top. Bake 15-18 minutes, or until lightly browned.

Tips and Variations

Wrap individual leftover muffins in plastic wrap and store in a Ziploc bag in the freezer. To reheat, remove the plastic wrap and wrap in a paper towel. Microwave in high for 30-60 seconds. Muffins will keep for up to one month in the freezer.

Coffee Cakes & Pastries

Coffee Cakes & Pastries

> "There are few hours in life more agreeable than the hour dedicated to the ceremony known as afternoon tea."
>
> —HENRY JAMES, *The Portrait of a Lady*

ASH STREET INN

This historic Amelia Island inn consists of two period homes that are combined to bring guests the ultimate in elegance and comfort. The main home, built in 1904, contains six luxuriously appointed guest rooms. The guesthouse was built in 1880 and houses the remaining four guest rooms. Each room features period antiques

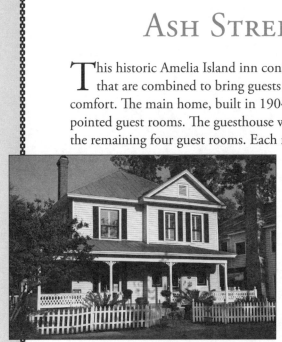

and complementing décor. Spa-quality bath products and fluffy robes come in each room. With complimentary daily refreshments, a heated pool and courtyard, wrap around porch, and spa treatment, Ash Street is certainly a great place to get away from it all. Plus, the innkeepers at the Ash Street Inn are dedicated to providing guests with the best accommodation possible! So sit back and relax, leave all your worries at home, and enjoy your stay.

"Everything here was awesome. We really enjoyed such a hospitable environment. The staff was superb, the breakfast was delicious, and the massage and Jacuzzi – heaven on Earth! We will be back. We want to stay in a different room each time. Oh, yeah, yummy cookies, too!"

— GUEST

INNKEEPERS: Jill Dorsen Chi & Samuel Chi

ADDRESS: 102 South 7th Street, Amelia Island, Florida 32034

TELEPHONE: (904) 277-6660; (800) 277-6660

E-MAIL: ashstreetinn@yahoo.com

WEBSITE: www.ashstreetinn.net

ROOMS: 10 Rooms; Private baths

CHILDREN: Children age 5 and older welcome; Call ahead

PETS: Small pets welcome; Resident pet

Almond Skillet Coffee Cake

Makes 16 Servings

"We call it dessert for breakfast and our guests just love it. This is a dense, flavorful torte that will wow 'em every time. We give out this recipe more than any other because the beauty of it is that it's easy!"

— *INNKEEPER, Ash Street Inn*

¾ cup melted butter
1½ cups sugar
　　plus ¼ cup for sprinkling on top
2 eggs
1½ cups flour
Pinch of salt
1 teaspoon almond extract
½ cup slivered almonds

Preheat oven to 350°F. In a medium bowl, combine the butter and 1½ cups sugar; mix well. Add the eggs, 1 at a time, mixing well after each addition. Add the flour, salt, and almond extract and mix to combine. Line a cast-iron skillet with aluminum foil, extending over the side; spray foil with non-stick cooking spray. Turn the batter out into the prepared skillet. Sprinkle with almonds and ¼ cup sugar. Bake 30-35 minutes, or until a toothpick inserted in the center comes away clean.

Cool completely before serving.

CASA DE ROSA

The magical Casa de Rosa is an Italian inspired villa right in West Palm Beach. Built in 1926, the building has proved to be the perfect setting for Elaine and Frank Calendrillo's beautiful bed & breakfast. Every aspect of the inn's design is meant to enhance each guest's comfort and helps to provide a memorable and enjoyable vacation experience. From the lush gardens and heated pool to the elegant and cozy guestrooms, each detail has been carefully selected. Guests will delight in the old world charm. Of course, even in an old world setting, every convenience is still available.

The immaculate gardens provide a great place for a relaxing afternoon and who doesn't crave a dip in their magnificent pool. In the afternoon, you can take a trip into town and visit some of West Palm Beach's best shopping and dining. There are also a host of year-round festivals to attend. Visit the South Florida Science Museum, the Palm Beach Zoo, or the Norton Museum of Art before returning to the inn for a rejuvenating night's sleep.

INNKEEPERS: Elaine & Frank Calendrillo

ADDRESS: 520 27th Street, West Palm Beach, Florida 33407

TELEPHONE: (561) 833-1920; (888) 665-8666

E-MAIL: Elaine@casaderosa.com

WEBSITE: www.casaderosa.com

ROOMS: 3 Rooms; 1 Cottage; Private baths

CHILDREN: Children age 12 and older welcome

PETS: Not allowed

Lemon Tea Cake

Makes 1 Cake

"This recipe was one of many handed down to me from my Aunt Sarah. She was a wonderful baker."

—INNKEEPER, *Casa de Rose*

2¼ cups flour
½ teaspoon salt
½ teaspoon baking soda
1 cup soft butter
2 cups sugar
3 eggs
1 teaspoon vanilla extract
1 teaspoon grated lemon rind
1 (8 ounce) container sour cream

Glaze:
1 cup confectioners sugar
1-2 teaspoons lemon juice

Preheat oven to 325°F; grease and flour a tube or bundt pan. In a medium bowl, sift together the flour, salt, and baking soda. In a large bowl, combine the butter, sugar, eggs, vanilla, lemon rind, and sour cream. Add the dry ingredients to the wet mixture and blend together, using an electric mixer on medium speed, about 3 minutes. Pour the batter into the prepared cake pan and bake 60-70 minutes.

Allow the cake to cool a bit before removing from the pan. Cool completely before topping with glaze.

For the glaze: Mix together the confectioners sugar and lemon juice to make a glaze of desired consistency. Using a fork, poke holes in top of the cooled cake so that the glaze can be easily absorbed. Pour the glaze over and serve

Sticky Buns

Plan ahead, this dish needs to refrigerate overnight!

Makes 8 Servings

*"This recipe was handed down from
my Aunt Sarah who was a fabulous baker."*
—INNKEEPER, *Casa de Rosa*

Dough:
1 package yeast
1 cup warm water
¼ cup sugar
1 teaspoon salt
2 tablespoons melted butter
1 egg, room temperature
3½ - 4 cups flour

Nut Mixture:
½ cup melted butter
½ cup brown sugar
1 tablespoon light corn syrup
⅔ cup chopped walnuts or pecans

Filling:
2 tablespoons softened butter
½ cup sugar
2 teaspoons cinnamon
Raisins (optional)

For the dough: Dissolve the yeast in warm water for 3 minutes. Add the remaining dough ingredients, mixing to combine. Knead the dough and place in a greased bowl; refrigerate overnight.

The following morning: Place the ingredients for the nut mixture into the bottom of a greased 13x9-inch baking dish. On a floured surface, to prevent sticking, roll the dough out into a rectangle. Spread the filling ingredients over the dough. Roll the dough from the long end of the rectangle up. Cut into 1-inch slices and place on top of the nut mixture, cover with a damp cloth and let rise in a warm place 1½ hours.

Preheat oven to 350°F and bake 25-30 minutes.

STICKY BUNS are similar to cinnamon rolls in that they consist of rolled pieces of dough, usually spread with brown sugar and cinnamon, that are sliced into rounds. Here is where they differ, however. The sticky bun is pressed into a baking dish that has been lined with ingredients like syrup or honey, and nuts – the "sticky" part of the sticky bun. After the buns have baked, they are inverted so that the sticky part is now the top of the bun.

These tasty pastries appear to have evolved directly from the German schnecken. Similar pastries include the butterhorn and the rugelach. The main difference between a schnecken and a rugelach, though, is that the schnecken dough typically contains sour cream and the rugelach dough contains cream cheese. Whether you roll a schnecken like a crescent roll or like a cinnamon roll is up for debate, but they're sure to be good either way.

Inn Shepard's Park B&B

Located in Stuart, Florida is the quaint and charming Inn Shepard's Park B&B. Hostess Marilyn Miller has created an intimate and elegant bed and breakfast with all the perks. Breakfast is a traditional Continental featuring an assortment of muffins, breads, and danishes. The inn is a comfortable retreat nestled in the heart of historic Stuart and just minutes from a host of attractions. Take a walk amongst the town's art galleries and shops, dine at one of many restaurants, and enjoy local music downtown.

Marin County and Hutchison beaches are close by, as are private and semi-private golf courses, recreation and environmental centers, and area parks. You may not know, but Stuart is known as the Sailfish Capital. Appropriately, inland and offshore boating and fishing are two of the area's biggest attractions.

INNKEEPERS: Marilyn Miller

ADDRESS: 601 SW Ocean Blvd, Stuart, Florida 34994

TELEPHONE: (772) 781-4244

E-MAIL: marilyn@innshepard.com

WEBSITE: www.innshepard.com

ROOMS: 4 Rooms; Private & shared baths

CHILDREN: Children age 12 and older welcome

PETS: Dogs welcome; Resident pets

CREAM CHEESE DANISH

Makes 8 Servings

2 (8 ounce) cans crescent rolls
2 (8-ounce) packages cream cheese
¾ cup sugar
1 teaspoon vanilla extract
1 teaspoon lemon juice
1 egg yolk, reserve egg white

Glaze:
Confectioners sugar
Vanilla extract
Lemon juice

Preheat oven to 350°F. Press 1 can of crescent rolls into the bottom of a small cookie sheet with sides. Roll the second can of crescent rolls between sheets of plastic wrap until the dough is the same size as the pressed crescent layer on the cookie sheet; set aside. In a medium bowl, beat together the cream cheese, sugar, vanilla, lemon, and egg yolk. Spread the mixture over the crescent roll layer on the cookie sheet. Remove the plastic wrap from the second layer of crescent roll dough and place the dough over the cream cheese layer. Press sides together to seal. Brush with the reserved egg white and bake 25-30 minutes, until the top is browned.

To serve: Cut into desired size and sprinkle with powdered sugar or spread with glaze.

For the glaze: Mix a bit of lemon juice and vanilla extract into about ½ cup of confectioners sugar until you have a glaze of desired consistency. Amounts will vary according to taste and consistency.

LONGBOARD INN AND NUNS & ROSES

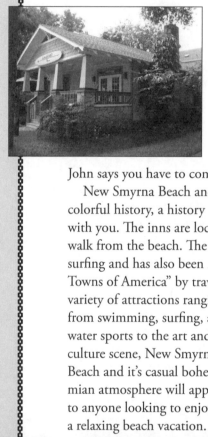

Longboard Inn and Nuns & Roses are two inns located in New Smyrna Beach, practically catty-corner to one another. The Longboard is a craftsman-style cottage that perfectly reflects the relaxed and casual personalities of owners John & Dee Green. Nuns & Roses is an elegant Victorian that is also known as the Rose Villa. Why Nuns, though? John says you have to come and find out for yourself.

New Smyrna Beach and the Longboard Inn share a long and colorful history, a history that John and Dee will happily share with you. The inns are located in the historic district, just a short walk from the beach. The town is nationally renowned for its great surfing and has also been rated one of the top fifty "Best Small Art Towns of America" by travel writer John Villani. With its wide variety of attractions ranging from swimming, surfing, and water sports to the art and culture scene, New Smyrna Beach and it's casual bohemian atmosphere will appeal to anyone looking to enjoy a relaxing beach vacation.

INNKEEPERS: John & Dee Green

ADDRESS: 312 Washington Street, New Smyrna Beach, Florida 32168

TELEPHONE: (386) 428-3499; (888) 655-2025

E-MAIL: info@longboardinn.com

WEBSITE: www.longboardinn.com

ROOMS: 6 Suites; 2 Cottages; Private baths

CHILDREN: Children age 12 and older welcome

PETS: Welcome; Resident pets

Orange Scones

Makes 2 "Loaves"

2½ cups flour
½ cup sugar
4 teaspoons baking powder
½ teaspoon baking soda
½ cup butter, softened
1 cup dried cranberries or chopped apricots
3 teaspoons grated orange peel
1 cup plain yogurt
½ teaspoon salt
1 teaspoon vanilla extract
1 teaspoon orange extract
⅔ cup buttermilk, or regular milk

Preheat oven to 375°F. Grease two cookie sheets and set aside. In a large bowl, combine the flour, sugar, baking powder, and baking soda. Cut in the butter and mix with a fork or pastry blender until mixture is coarse and crumbly. Add the cranberries (or apricots) and 2 teaspoons of the orange peel to the mixture. Add the yogurt, salt, extracts, and buttermilk and mix to combine. Shape the dough into two balls and place one on each cookie sheet. Pat dough down lightly and brush with buttermilk. Sprinkle the remaining orange peel over the top and bake 15-20 minutes, or until golden brown.

Cut into wedges and serve with vanilla/orange cream cheese spread.

THE OLD PINEAPPLE INN

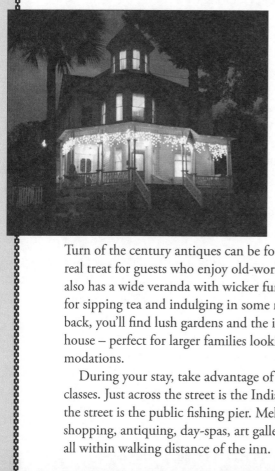

Nestled beneath grand oaks and Spanish moss sits the enchanting and historic Old Pineapple Inn. The home was originally built in the late 1800s and remained in the hands of the same family until 1995. Now on the National Register of Historic Places, this quaint inn provides a relaxed and intimate lodging experience for visitors to Melbourne. Turn of the century antiques can be found throughout the inn, a real treat for guests who enjoy old-world charm and history. The inn also has a wide veranda with wicker furniture and porch swing great for sipping tea and indulging in some much needed relaxation. Out back, you'll find lush gardens and the inn's pool as well as the guest house – perfect for larger families looking for longer-term accommodations.

During your stay, take advantage of the inn's gourmet cooking classes. Just across the street is the Indian River Lagoon and down the street is the public fishing pier. Melbourne also has great dining, shopping, antiquing, day-spas, art galleries, and specialty boutiques, all within walking distance of the inn.

INNKEEPER: Celeste Henry

ADDRESS: 1736 Pineapple Avenue, Melbourne, Florida 32935

TELEPHONE: (321) 254-1347; (888) 776-9864

E-MAIL: innkeepers@oldpineappleinn.com

WEBSITE: www.oldpineappleinn.com

ROOMS: 3 Rooms; 1 Cottage; Private baths

CHILDREN: Welcome

PETS: Not allowed

Almond Apricot Scones

Makes 8 Scones

"Everyone is always so surprised by how soft and light these scones are."

—Innkeeper, *The Old Pineapple Inn*

2 cups sifted flour, white or soft wheat
¼ cup sugar
3 teaspoons baking powder
¼ teaspoon salt
⅓ cup butter, at room temperature
2 eggs, at room temperature
½ cup heavy cream
½ cup chopped dried apricots
1 teaspoon almond extract

Optional:
Sliced almonds
Raw sugar crystals

Preheat oven to 400°F. In a medium bowl, sift together the flour, sugar, baking powder, and salt. Cut in the butter until the mixture is fine crumbs. In a small bowl, beat together 1 whole egg and 1 egg yolk, reserving the white for brushing the tops of the scones. Add the eggs, cream, almond extract, and apricots to the dry ingredients to form a soft dough. Stir until just moistened, do not overmix.

Knead the dough five or six times and then form small rounds about ½-inch thick. Beat the reserved egg white slightly and brush over the tops of the scones. Sprinkle with sliced almonds and raw sugar if desired. Transfer the scones to an ungreased baking sheet, spaced about 1-inch apart. Bake 15 minutes. Serve hot or at room temperature with butter, crème fraiche, or lemon curd.

Cedar Key B&B

This sprawling inn in Cedar Key, Florida began life in 1880 as the home of one of the heads of the Eagle Pencil Company. The building also served as residence for any visitors and guests of the company as well. In 1900, the home was converted to a boarding house that was run by the daughter of Florida's first senator. Innkeepers, Bill and Alice Phillips, purchased the home in 2003 after it had been converted to a bed & breakfast.

Today, the inn features seven elegantly appointed guest rooms and an additional two suites, each with it's own distinctive décor. Cedar Key B&B is also conveniently located just steps from the Gulf of Mexico. Wake each morning to lovely Gulf views and a scrumptious homemade breakfast. Alice & Bill are happy to share any recipes as well! Then take a walk to the beach or to Cedar Key's gift shops, art galleries, and museums. Eat at one of the gourmet seafood restaurants, take in some kayaking, or sit back and enjoy a carriage ride through town. Boat tours and fishing charters are also available, just ask Bill & Alice for the best offers in town. Cedar Key is also a great retreat for nature lovers. Bird watching is quite popular in the area and the Lower Suwannee Wildlife Refuge is a great place to take a scenic hike or canoe trip.

INNKEEPERS: Alice & Bill Phillips

ADDRESS: 810 3rd Street, Cedar Key, Florida 32625

TELEPHONE: (352) 543-9000; (877) 543-9171

E-MAIL: info@cedarkeybandb.com

WEBSITE: www.cedarkeybandb.com

ROOMS: 7 Rooms; 2 Suites; Private baths

CHILDREN: Welcome; Call ahead

PETS: Welcome; Resident pets

Blueberry Scones

Makes 1 Dozen

*"These are nice, light, and fluffy, unlike the "brick" type scones
you so often get. Our guests absolutely love these!"*
—INNKEEPER, *Cedar Key B&B*

3 cups flour
2 teaspoons baking powder
½ cup sugar
Pinch salt
1 pint blueberries
Zest of 3 lemons
2 cups heavy cream

Preheat oven to 350°F. In a large bowl, sift together the flour,
baking powder, sugar, and salt. Add in the blueberries and lemon
zest and fluff together with a fork. Pour in the heavy cream and
use two forks to *gently* blend the cream into the flour/blueberry
mixture. Do not overwork the dough. Form into scones of desired
size adding extra flour if needed. Bake 25 minutes.

Tips and Variations

The shaped dough will freeze very well.
When baking from frozen, bake 30 minutes.

Palms & Roses B&B

Palms & Roses is a great place to settle in and enjoy some peace and quiet. The inn is located just ten miles from Ocala and a short drive from six different natural springs. Local lakes are great for bass fishing and there's also world-class golfing nearby. Then, of course, there's Orlando and Daytona Beach. About an hour's drive takes you right to the Disney parks or the Daytona Speedway. There's also dining and shopping just fifteen minutes from the inn. Though the inn is never far from any of these attractions, it's still a hidden oasis perfect for relaxing and spending some time alone with that special someone. A full English breakfast is served daily and you can always kick back and lounge by the fabulous indoor pool. If you do decide to venture out for the day, this home away from home will be waiting for you when you return.

"My wife and I were looking for a peaceful retreat from the BUSY-ness of life and found rest at Palms & Roses. My wife lived in England for a few years and loved the conversations with Jenni. She and Don are wonderful and gracious hosts. The covered pool is a delight, the room was very clean, and the shower was huge! If you are traveling in Central Florida and want to escape to some serenity (and eat an awesome British breakfast), you've found the best b&b for it." —GUEST

INNKEEPERS: Donald & Jennifer Kehl
ADDRESS: 15065 SE 73rd Avenue, Summerfield, Florida 34491
TELEPHONE: (352) 245-9022
E-MAIL: palmsandroses@gmail.com
WEBSITE: www.palmsandroses.com
ROOMS: 3 Suites; Private baths
CHILDREN: Cannot Accommodate
PETS: Welcome; Call ahead; Resident Pets

Raspberry Buns

Makes 12 Servings

*"This recipe is out of a recipe book that came with
a new oven delivered around 1940 in the UK."*
—INNKEEPER, *Palms & Roses*

1 cup flour
$1/3$ cup butter
$1/3$ cup sugar
1 teaspoon baking powder
1 egg
Rind from one lemon, grated
Milk
Raspberry jam

Preheat oven to 325°F. In a medium bowl, rub the butter into
the flour to form a sandy mixture. Add the sugar, baking powder,
egg, lemon rind, and enough milk to form a stiff paste. Form the
mixture into small balls and make a hole in the center of each. Fill
the center with raspberry jam and pinch the hole closed. Place the
filled buns on a greased cookie sheet and bake for 25 minutes.

Vanilla Slices

Makes 12 Servings

½ pound puff pastry
Vanilla extract
½ pint (1 cup) thick custard
Prepared icing of choice

Preheat oven to 350°F. Roll the puff pastry out to about ⅛-inch thickness and cut into two strips 4 ½ inches wide and as long as the pastry will allow. Place the pastry on a baking sheet and bake 14 minutes.

While the pastry is baking, add a few drops of vanilla to the prepared custard. When the pastry has cooled, spread the custard on one strip and cover with the second. Cover with icing and cut into 2-inch pieces to serve.

Tips and Variations

Variation: Try a mixture of heavy cream and raspberry jam in place of the custard. Fruit jam combined with softened cream cheese will also work.

If you are using custard, these will freeze very well and can be prepared ahead of time.

PHYLLO DOUGH is a paper-thin sheet of raw, unleavened flour dough, that is usually found in Greek and Middle Eastern cooking. Homemade phyllo is an art, but today you can readily find these delicate sheets of pastry in any grocer's freezer. Some other uses for the dough include:

Austrian Apfelstrudel – phyllo stuffed with apples, cinnamon, and raisins

Turkish Peynirli Borek – layered with cheese

Moroccan Bstilla – shredded chicken and spices in a phyllo crust

Greek Baklava – layers of phyllo with nuts and syrup or honey

Bulgarian Patatnik – phyllo stuffed with potatoes

French Toast, Pancakes, Waffles, & Crêpes

French Toast, Pancakes, Waffles, & Crêpes

THE OLD POWDER HOUSE INN

Breakfast at the Old Powder House Inn has earned rave reviews from returning guests. Now you can try a taste of it yourself. Katie has graciously shared the recipe for her house specialty, Stuffed French Toast. Complimentary coffee, tea, cold drinks, and home-made baked treats are available for guests throughout the day. There is also an afternoon tea, dessert, and a wine and cheese service. The Old Powder House Inn is a delight for all of your senses, especially the palate!

'The Old Powder House Inn is a wonderful bed and breakfast experience. The owners, Kal and Katie, are such warm and gracious hosts; we felt at home and we felt pampered. The inn is beautifully decorated, each room is unique and charming... The breakfasts are delicious! My personal favorite is the stuffed French toast. We also enjoyed sitting on the veranda in the evening watching the horse drawn carriages drive by... If you are looking for a special place to stay, The Old Powder House is that place..." — GUEST

INNKEEPERS: **Katie & Kal Kalieta**

ADDRESS: **38 Cordova Street, St. Augustine, Florida 32084**

TELEPHONE: **(904) 824-4149; (800) 447-4149**

E-MAIL: **innkeeper@oldpowderhouse.com**

WEBSITE: **www.oldpowderhouse.com**

ROOMS: **9 Rooms; 2 Suites; Private baths**

CHILDREN: **Children age 8 and older welcome**

PETS: **Not allowed**

Katie's Famous Almond French Toast

Plan ahead, this dish needs to be refrigerated overnight!
Makes 8 Servings

1 loaf French bread, frozen
6 ounces cream cheese, softened
$\frac{1}{3}$ cup apricot and
    pineapple preserves
6 eggs
1 tablespoon vanilla extract

1 tablespoon cinnamon
$\frac{1}{8}$ teaspoon nutmeg
½ cup heavy whipping cream
½ cup milk
1 stick butter

Remove the frozen bread from the freezer about 10 minutes before you are ready to begin preparation. Slice the loaf into 1-inch slices and cut a pocket ¾ of the way through each slice. In a small bowl, mix together the cream cheese and preserves. Put 2 tablespoons of the mixture into each pocket. In a medium bowl, mix the eggs, vanilla, cinnamon, nutmeg, cream, and milk. Dip the stuffed bread slices into the mixture and place on a greased 9x13-onch baking dish. Spoon remaining egg mixture over the top of the sandwiches. Cover and refrigerate overnight.

The following morning: Remove the dish from the refrigerator at least 45 minutes before baking. Preheat oven to 375°F. Melt the butter in the microwave and spoon about 1 tablespoon over each sandwich. Flip and repeat on other side. Bake 8-10 minutes until golden brown, flip each sandwich and bake an additional 5 minutes. Remove from oven and serve with your favorite sauce or syrup (almond sauce recommended).

For the almond sauce: In a heavy saucepan heat 1 cup granulated sugar with 1 cup corn syrup until blended, about 5 minutes on medium heat. Add 1 cup heavy cream and blend to mix, heat to simmer – do not boil. Remove from heat and stir in 1 tablespoon almond extract. Allow the sauce to cool and pour into storage containers. Freezes well!

Tips and Variations

Variation: To make Strawberry Cinnamon Bread instead, use cinnamon raisin bread or brown sugar and cinnamon bread in place of white bread. Follow recipe as above but substitute strawberry preserves in place of the apricot and pineapple. You can also mix fresh strawberries and banana slices into the cream cheese if you like. Serve with heated strawberry preserves and whipped cream.

Turtle Beach Inn & Cottages at Indian Pass

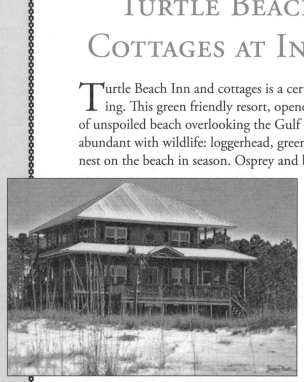

Turtle Beach Inn and cottages is a certified Florida Green Lodging. This green friendly resort, opened in 1997, sits on a stretch of unspoiled beach overlooking the Gulf of Mexico. The area is abundant with wildlife: loggerhead, green, and leatherback turtles nest on the beach in season. Osprey and bald eagles fly by overhead and families of dolphins can be seen swimming past. And, if you rent a kayak the dolphins will swim right up to you!

If peace and solitude are what you seek, Turtle Beach Inn is definitely the place for you. Town is just a fifteen-minute drive so you're never far from restaurants or shopping, but you can relax and enjoy the quiet without worrying about sharing your retreat.

INNKEEPER:	Trish Petrie
ADDRESS:	140 Painted Pony Road, Port St. Joe, Florida 32456
TELEPHONE:	(850) 229-9366
E-MAIL:	info@turtlebeachinn.com
WEBSITE:	www.turtlebeachinn.com
ROOMS:	4 Rooms; 3 Cottages; Private & shared baths
CHILDREN:	Welcome; Call ahead
PETS:	Not allowed; Resident pets

Baked French Toast

Plan ahead, this dish needs to be refrigerated overnight!
Makes 8-10 Servings

"This recipe was given to me by one of our guests.
It has since become Turtle Beach Inn's signature dish.
It's very popular especially on Sunday mornings!"
—INNKEEPER, *Turtle Beach Inn*

1 stick butter
1 tablespoon corn syrup
1 cup brown sugar
1 pound twin French bread loaves
5 whole eggs
1½ cups milk
1 teaspoon cinnamon

In a small saucepan over medium heat, mix the butter, syrup, and sugar; simmer one minute. Pour the mixture into a 9x13-inch baking dish. Slice the French bread into ¾-inch thick slices and layer over the brown sugar mixture. Beat the eggs in a medium bowl and add in the milk and cinnamon. Pour the mixture over the bread. Cover the dish and refrigerate overnight.

The following morning: Preheat oven to 350°F. Uncover the dish and bake 40 minutes, or until browned and puffed.

Night Swan Intracoastal B&B

The three-story, circa 1906 Night Swan Intracoastal is a romantic and memorable vacation spot. Night Swan has fifteen guest rooms, each with king or queen beds, cozy linens, complimentary robes, and many with Jacuzzi tubs. And the views are to die for.

From your room you can enjoy the sights and sounds of the ocean. You can also walk out on the inn's 140-foot dock and sit watching the pelicans fly over head and the dolphins swim by. For those cooler evenings, enjoy a hot coffee while sitting on the wrap-around porch or the front room and watch the sunrise with your special someone.

The central location of this inn, between Daytona Beach and the Kennedy Space Center, is great for travelers looking to experience the best that Florida has to offer. Enjoy a sunset cruise, try some deep-sea or fly-fishing, play golf on world-class courses, and relax on the white sandy beaches. A short trip into town finds great shops, art galleries, and restaurants. Just ask Martha and Chuck for some suggestions and you're on your way. Whether you want the full tourist experience or a beach-side romantic retreat, Night Swan is perfect for both.

INNKEEPERS: Martha & Chuck Nighswonger
ADDRESS: 512 South Riverside Drive, New Smyrna Beach, FL 32168
TELEPHONE: (386) 423-4940; (800) 465-4261
E-MAIL: info@nightswan.com
WEBSITE: www.nightswan.com
ROOMS: 12 Rooms; 3 Suites; Private baths
CHILDREN: Welcome
PETS: Welcome

Oven-Baked French Toast

Makes 2 Servings

½ cup egg-whites (about 4-5 egg whites)
¼ cup skim milk
¼ teaspoon cinnamon
½ teaspoon vanilla extract
Dash of salt
6 slices day-old French bread
1 cup Rice Krispies cereal

In a shallow dish, whisk together the egg whites, skim milk, cinnamon, vanilla, and salt. Dip the bread slices in the egg mixture and drain off excess liquid. If you are using a dense bread, you can perform this step the night before and allow the bread to soak overnight.

Preheat oven to 450°F. Coat the bread slices with the Rice Krispies cereal. Place the coated bread on a buttered baking sheet and bake 6-7 minutes per side. Serve three slices per person.

CASA DE SUENOS

Casa de Suenos means House of Dreams. Owner Kathleen Hurley purchased this building in 2001 and converted the circa 1904 Mediterranean-style home into an inn that is truly a dream vacation spot for guests. Located in historic St. Augustine, Casa de Suenos lies right on the historic carriage route. Guests will delight in seeing horse drawn carriages that still pass the inn today. Shopping, dining, art galleries, and historic sightseeing are all just a short walk away and just five minutes will take you straight to the beach and a host of water activities.

Each of the inn's five rooms has been uniquely outfitted with a different décor and color scheme. Three of the five guestrooms feature whirlpool tubs and private balconies and all of the rooms come with compact refrigerators and a decanter of cream sherry. On Friday and Saturday evenings, Kathleen hosts a social hour with complimentary beverages and snacks. Each morning, guests enjoy a hearty gourmet breakfast.

INNKEEPER: Kathleen Hurley

ADDRESS: 20 Cordova Street, St. Augustine, Florida 32084

TELEPHONE: (904) 824-0887; (800) 824-0804

E-MAIL: dream@casadesuenos.com

WEBSITE: www.casadesuenos.com

ROOMS: 5 Rooms; Private baths

CHILDREN: Children age 13 and older welcome

PETS: Not allowed

Praline French Toast

Makes 8 Servings

"I have owned my bed & breakfast for 7 years. In the first year that I operated the inn, I had a lovely guest that visited from Atlanta. She was gracious enough to send me this recipe and said that it was a favorite of her mother's. She commented that her mom made this dish for lots of church socials and other functions, and that it was always a hit! My guests have been enjoying it ever since."

— INNKEEPER, *Casa de Suenos*

1 cup brown sugar
1 stick butter
2 tablespoons corn syrup
1½ cups pecans, chopped and halved
8 croissants, split
6 eggs, beaten
1½ cups milk
1 teaspoon vanilla extract
1 teaspoon almond extract
Pinch of salt

Preheat oven to 350°F. In a saucepan over low heat, melt together the sugar, butter, and corn syrup. Lightly grease two 9x9-inch baking dishes and divide the sugar mixture evenly between the pans. Sprinkle the chopped pecans over the sugar mixture and arrange the croissant halves over the pecans. In a medium bowl, beat together the eggs, milk, vanilla and almond extracts, and salt and pour over the croissants. Make sure all of the croissants in both pans are wet. Cover dish with foil* and bake 45 minutes. Remove from oven and cut each pan into 8 squares. Dust with powdered sugar and serve.

Tips and Variations

*At this point you can either bake the dish right away or refrigerate overnight. If you are refrigerating, make sure that you allow the dish to sit at room temperature for about 30 minutes before baking.

LA VERANDA

La Veranda welcomes travelers seeking old world charm and luxury accommodations in an urban setting. This grand home with its wraparound porch is a warm and inviting place located in the heart of popular St. Petersburg, Florida. Homey comfort and elegant décor, a full breakfast, complimentary beverages all day long, and all just minutes from downtown, what more could you ask for?

"Some places just remind you of another era and happier times, this is that kind of place... Nancy makes you feel right at home and the others are a riot. Everyone knows where to go – dining, beaches, etc. For all that, my favorite spot was sitting in a rocking chair on the veranda and enjoying the evening with a glass of wine... breakfast on the porch is a must. This is a true 'Old Florida' experience, just relax, put on your sandals and shorts, and enjoy yourself..." —GUEST

INNKEEPERS: Nancy Mayer & Jay Jones

ADDRESS: 111 5th Avenue N, St. Petersburg, Florida 33701

TELEPHONE: (727) 824-9997; (800) 484-8423, x8417

E-MAIL: info@laverandabb.com

WEBSITE: www.laverandabb.com

ROOMS: 2 Rooms; 3 Suites; Private baths

CHILDREN: Welcome

PETS: Welcome; Resident pet

Pecan Praline French Toast

Plan ahead, this dish needs to refrigerate overnight!
Makes 6-8 servings

1 loaf French bread
6 large eggs
$\frac{1}{8}$ teaspoon ground nutmeg
$\frac{1}{8}$ teaspoon cinnamon
1½ cups milk
1½ cups half & half
1 teaspoon vanilla extract

Topping:
½ cup softened butter
1 cup light brown sugar
2 tablespoons dark corn syrup
1 cup chopped pecans

Spray a 9x13-inch baking dish with non-stick cooking spray. Cut the French bread into medium slices and layer over the bottom of the pan – 2 layers. In a large bowl, mix together the eggs, nutmeg, cinnamon, milk, half & half, and vanilla extract. Pour the mixture over the bread layers, cover the dish, and refrigerate overnight.

The following morning: Preheat oven to 350°F. In a medium bowl, mix together the softened butter, brown sugar, corn syrup, and pecans for the topping. Spread the topping mixture over the bread and bake 40-45 minutes.

Pelican Path B&B
by the Sea

Every morning at the Pelican Path, Tom and Joan make a hearty and filling breakfast. Their ever-changing selection includes items like pancakes, waffles, French Toast, omelets, fresh fruit, juice, and homemade breads, coffee cakes, or muffins. Each room also comes with a mini-fridge that is kept stocked with a selection of soft drinks, juice, and bottle water.

"…Pelican Path is everything and more than what you will find on their website. I had a king room with Jacuzzi tub that was wonderful… The room was bright, cheery, and very large. The inn is located on a quiet part of the beach, which was just what I needed; the are is more residential than commercial. Towels, lounge chairs, and bikes are provided daily… The breakfasts were out of this world! I even got one of the recipes from Joan so I could serve it to my family. Joan and her husband, Tom, were a delight as well – never intrusive and always ready to please. My husband and I are planning to stay here next time we are both in [Jacksonville]. I would highly recommend this b&b to anyone visiting [Jacksonville Beach]." — GUEST

INNKEEPERS:	Joan & Tom Hubbard
ADDRESS:	11 North 19th Avenue, Jacksonville, Florida 32250
TELEPHONE:	(904) 249-1177; (888) 749-1177
E-MAIL:	ppbandb@aol.com
WEBSITE:	www.pelicanpath.com
ROOMS:	4 Rooms; Private baths
CHILDREN:	Cannot accommodate
PETS:	Not allowed

Delightfully Stuffed French Toast

Makes 6-8 Servings

"This recipe was given to us by our innsitters.
It's great because you can increase or decrease the recipe very easily
to suit the number of servings you need."
—INNKEEPER, *Pelican Path B&B by the Sea*

6-8 ounces cream cheese
2-3 tablespoons confectioners sugar
1 teaspoon vanilla extract
12-16 slices of bread
5-6 eggs
Milk

In a small bowl, mix together the cream cheese, confectioners sugar, and vanilla. Spread a thin layer of the mixture between two slices of bread to make a sandwich, repeat until you have 6-8 sandwiches. At this point, you can refrigerate the sandwiches overnight if you like.

When you are ready to cook, mix the eggs with a bit of milk to make a thin custard. Dunk both sides of each sandwich in the mixture before placing on a hot griddle or skillet over medium-high heat. Cook until lightly browned on both sides. Cut each sandwich in half and dust with confectioners sugar to serve. For a fancier presentation, add some sliced fruit on top of each sandwich.

Blueberry Supreme

Plan ahead, this dish needs to be refrigerated overnight!
Makes 8-10 Servings

*"This recipe was e-mailed to me by a guest who stayed with us.
I have increased the size to feed more people.
It is a breakfast favorite at Pelican Path."*
—INNKEEPER, *Pelican Path B&B by the Sea*

1 (12 ounce) container cream cheese
8 eggs
2 cups milk
1 cup half & half
¾ cup maple syrup
4 large croissants, cut in half length-wise
Canned blueberries (or fruit of choice)
Confectioners sugar

Sauce:
1 tablespoon cornstarch
1 tablespoon
  confectioners sugar
Liquid drained from
  canned blueberries

Mix the cream cheese in a large bowl until it is soft and creamy. Add the eggs one at a time, mixing with each addition. Add the milk, half & half, and syrup and mix until well blended. Grease a 9x12-inch baking dish and line with the croissant halves. Pour the cream cheese mixture over the top, cover the dish, and refrigerate overnight.

The following morning: Preheat oven to 375°F. Sprinkle the blueberries over the top of the casserole and bake 45-50 minutes. Dust with confectioners sugar to serve.

For the sauce topping: In a small saucepan over medium heat, mix together 1 tablespoon of cornstarch with a little water until smooth. Add the confectioners sugar and the liquid drained off the blueberries and stir together until thickened. Serve on the side as a topping option.

Tips and Variations

If you are using fresh blueberries or other fresh berries, you can still make the sauce, simply mash up extra berries to use in place of the canned liquid. Jarred preserves can also be used, simply cut the sugar to taste.

FRENCH TOAST came about as a great way to use up stale bread. The old bread was soaked in an egg mixture and then fried making the hard crusty bread into a silky concoction that's enjoyed all over the world. Whether you eat is sweet or savory, as breakfast or dessert, stuff it, fry it, or bake it, the idea is always the same.

Here are some ways other countries enjoy French Toast:

England: Eggy Bread – dipped in egg and milk, fried, and served with various sauces

Italy: Mozzarella in Carrozza – a mozzarella sandwich dipped in egg and fried

Spain: Torrijas – thick bread soaked in milk or wine, fried, and drenched in spiced honey

Portugal: Rabanadas – bread leftovers soaked in milk, dipped in egg, and fried in olive oil then dipped in sugar and cinnamon

GRADY HOUSE
BED & BREAKFAST

Grady House is a great place to relax and rejuvenate. Their wonderful gardens provide some of the best shade for afternoon naps or curling up with a good book, and the sumptuous beds are so comfy you may never want to get up in the morning. The smell of Lucie's homemade breakfast is sure to entice you, though! After a hearty meal, you'll be ready for a day of adventure or leisure, whichever you choose. Nearby state parks and natural springs provide wonderful snorkeling and diving opportunities. There's also canoe and kayak rentals or even tubing down the river. For all you shoppers out there, High Springs was once known as the antique capital. If you do decide to stay in, consider treating yourself to a spa day next door.

"My husband and I spent two nights at Grady House – one night in the Yellow Room and the second in the Navy room. Both were very comfortable and beautifully decorated. The owners are extremely friendly and helpful, they make every effort to make your stay enjoyable and comfortable. The breakfast was stupendous and the large gardens behind the home are perfect for relaxing with a glass of wine after a hard day floating down the Ichenetucknee River!" — GUEST

INNKEEPERS: Paul & Lucie Regensdorf
ADDRESS: 420 NW 1st Avenue, High Springs, FL 32643
TELEPHONE: (386) 454-2206
E-MAIL: gradyhouse@gradyhouse.com
WEBSITE: www.gradyhouse.com
ROOMS: 2 Rooms; 3 Suites; 1 Cottage
CHILDREN: Children age 10 and older welcome
PETS: Not allowed; Resident pets

Croissant French Toast with Blueberry Sauce

Makes 6 Servings

3 tablespoons butter
6 large eggs
¾ cup milk
1 teaspoon ground cinnamon
1 teaspoon vanilla extract
6 large croissants

Blueberry Sauce:
1 (16 ounce) package frozen blueberries
5 tablespoons sugar
1 tablespoon cornstarch
¼ cup plus 1 tablespoon water

Preheat a large non-stick skillet or griddle and spread with 1 tablespoon of butter. In a large bowl, whisk together the eggs, milk, cinnamon, and vanilla. Dip each croissant half in the egg mixture and turn to coat. Add as many croissants as will fit into the skillet and cook until lightly browned, turning once, about 2 minutes per side. Remove croissants from skillet and keep them warm until serving. Add the remaining butter to the skillet and repeat with remaining croissants. Serve topped with blueberry sauce.

For the blueberry sauce: Add the frozen blueberries, sugar, cornstarch, and water to a medium saucepan over medium-high heat; cook stirring frequently. Check for sweetness and add additional sugar if the mixture is too tart. Once the sugar has melted, add 1 tablespoon of water to the mixture. Purée ⅓-½ of the blueberry mixture in a food processor; return to pot and serve warm sauce over French toast.

River Park Inn B&B

In the 1880s, River Park Inn was a cottage for the "more retiring guests" of the Clarendon Hotel. The Cottage was run by Dr. Joseph Applegate, a partner of the Clarendon who owned the rights to the nearby mineral springs. As part of his "practice" Dr. Applegate prescribed the waters and dispensed bottles of it to wealthy guests. Although the inn no longer prescribes the waters today, the springs still flow at an amazing 3,000 gallons per minute and a comfortable

78°F and feed directly into the community pool. Pat recommends that guests take advantage and enjoy a "chemical free swim" while staying at the River Park Inn.

After Dr. Applegate's reign, the cottage served many different purposes. It has been a private residence, a boarding house, and even an antique store. River Park Inn has been fully renovated and restored with vintage and antique décor, high ceilings, and heart pine flooring. Each of the five guest rooms features tasteful and elegant furnishings and linens and has its own unique character and theme. The inn also has a common parlor where guests can sit by the fire on colder days, and wide, open porches and a veranda with swings and rockers.

INNKEEPER: Pat Sickles

ADDRESS: 103 South Magnolia Avenue, Green Cove Springs, FL 32043

TELEPHONE: (904) 284-2994; (888) 417-0363

E-MAIL: riverparkinn@comcast.net

WEBSITE: www.riverparkinn.com

ROOMS: 5 Rooms; Private baths

CHILDREN: Children age 2 and older welcome

PETS: Not allowed; Resident pets

Blueberry French Toast

Plan ahead, this dish needs to be refrigerated overnight!
Makes 1 Pie

"We like to serve this dish with fresh juice, sausage or bacon, scrambled eggs, and grits. Try substituting whole wheat bread, low-fat cream cheese, and egg beaters, to make this a more health conscious dish."
—INNKEEPER, *River Park Inn B&B*

10 ounces day-old bread
4 ounces cream cheese,
    frozen so you can easily cut
1 cup blueberries, fresh or frozen
6 eggs
1 cup milk
½ cup syrup, or more to taste

Grease* a 9-inch deep-dish pie plate. Cut the bread into cubes (you can remove the crusts but it is not necessary) and place half the bread cubes in the bottom of the greased dish. Cut the cream cheese into cubes and layer it over the bread. Top with the blueberries and the remaining bread cubes. In a large bowl, beat together the eggs, milk, and syrup; pour over the layered bread mixture, cover with foil, and refrigerate overnight.

The following morning: Preheat oven to 350°F and bake the French toast for 30 minutes. Uncover the dish and bake an additional 30 minutes, until the dish is golden brown and the center is firmly set. Turn the French toast out on a round serving dish and slice into pie slices, garnish with fresh fruit and serve!

Tips and Variations

*Innkeeper recommends a product called Release. It allows you to easily invert the dish over a serving platter without any mess! You can make this yourself using a mixture of equal parts shortening, flour, and oil (not olive). Brush the mixture over the inside of your pan and you're set.

Amelia Island Williams House

This elegant inn is two historic homes that were each part of the Williams family estate. Amelia Island Williams House was originally built in 1856 and was occupied by the Williams family for 100 years. Hearthstone Williams House was built in 1859 and features a one-of-a-kind gingerbread façade commissioned by Marcellus Williams and designed by architect Robert S. Schuyler. Past and present coexist in this unique historic inn, the only one of its kind in Fernandina Beach.

Every morning, you'll wake to the wonderful smells of a two-course gourmet breakfast. You may want to spend your afternoon relaxing in the luscious English garden and enjoying a glass of iced tea. 500-year-old live oaks, fountains, and a Japanese Koi pond provide a peaceful and serene setting. You could also head over to the beach for a day in the sun. Wine and hors d'oeuvres are served at the inn each evening at sunset and you can even arrange a romantic picnic on the beach or in the park.

INNKEEPERS: Deborah & Byron McCutchen

ADDRESS: 103 South Ninth Street, Amelia Island, Florida 32034

TELEPHONE: (904) 277-2328; (800) 414-9258

E-MAIL: info@williamshouse.com

WEBSITE: www.williamshouse.com

ROOMS: 10 Rooms; Private baths

CHILDREN: Children age 10 and older welcome

PETS: Not allowed

Blueberry Strata

Plan ahead, this dish needs to be refrigerated overnight!
Makes 12 Servings

*"Guests love this — they just can't believe how good
this unique blend of ingredients is!"*
—INNKEEPER, *Amelia Island Williams House*

> 1 loaf French bread, cut into 1-inch cubes
> 2 (8 ounce) packages cream cheese, cubed
> 1 cup fresh blueberries
> 12 large eggs
> $1/3$ cup maple syrup
> 2 cups whole milk

Spray a 9x13-inch baking dish with non-stick cooking spray.
Fill the bottom of the dish with half of the cubed bread. Scatter
the cream cheese and blueberries over the bread. Top with the
remaining bread cubes. In a medium bowl, combine the eggs,
syrup, and milk and pour over the entire mixture. Press down the
bread to absorb the egg mixture. Cover and refrigerate overnight.

The following morning: Preheat oven to 350°F. Cover dish with
foil and bake 30 minutes. Remove the foil and bake an additional
30 minutes.

To serve: Cut strata into squares. Sprinkle each square with
powdered sugar and drizzle with additional syrup.

CARRIAGE WAY B&B

With it's grand historic building, romantic atmosphere, and the hosts' attention to every detail, it's easy to see why the Carriage Way Bed & Breakfast was voted one of *Florida Monthly Magazine's* Best Three Bed & Breakfasts in Florida and was also picked one of Fodor's "Choices." Nestled in the heart of historic St. Augustine, the inn is the picture of elegance. Just moments from anything and everything you might want to do. You can wake each morning with breakfast in bed and then borrow one of the inn's beach bicycles for your day's adventures. In the afternoon, the inn serves up a special dessert treat for guests and complimentary beverages are available throughout the day. With all this, the inn maintains a casual and leisure air that will appeal to every guest.

"We had a terrific time here. [Our hosts] were incredibly friendly, gracious, and accommodating. Without a doubt the best b&b we've stayed at and we've been doing our 'girls' getaway' for 12 years now! We'll definitely be back. The food was great and plentiful, the room immaculate." — GUEST

INNKEEPERS:	Bill Johnson & sons, Larry & John
ADDRESS:	70 Cuna Street, St. Augustine, Florida 32084
TELEPHONE:	(904) 829-2467; (800) 908-9832
E-MAIL:	info@carriageway.com
WEBSITE:	www.carriageway.com
ROOMS:	11 Rooms; 1 Cottage; Private baths
CHILDREN:	Children age 8 and older welcome
PETS:	Not allowed

Blueberry Stuffed French Toast

Plan ahead, this dish needs to be refrigerated overnight!
Makes 12 Servings

*"This is Diane Johnson's signature breakfast dish
and has been served here for the past 16 years."*
—INNKEEPER, *Carriage Way B&B*

12 slices bakery bread, cubed
2 (8 ounce) packages cream cheese, cubed
1½ cups blueberries, fresh or frozen
1/2 cup maple syrup
10 eggs, beaten
2 cups milk
1 teaspoon vanilla extract

Topping:
1 cup sugar
2 tablespoons cornstarch
1 cup water
1½ cups blueberries

Layer half of the bread in the bottom of a 13x9-inch baking dish.
Top with all of the cubed cream cheese, the blueberries, and the
remaining bread. In a medium bowl, mix together the maple
syrup, eggs, milk, and vanilla; pour mixture over the layered dish.
Cover and refrigerate overnight.

The following morning: Preheat oven to 350°F. Bake covered
for 45 minutes, then uncovered for an addition 30 minutes. Let
stand 15 minutes before serving.

For the topping: Mix the sugar, cornstarch, and water together in
a saucepan over medium-high heat. Bring to a boil and add the
blueberries. Simmer 5 minutes and serve on the side.

MANATEE POCKET INN

This charming small-town inn is a lovely retreat located in the historic fishing village of Port Salerno. Named for the inland bay, Manatee Pocket, the inn has a refreshingly casual and laid-back atmosphere that is a trademark of the Florida Keys. Each of the inn's five guest rooms has a signature theme and complementing décor.

From the Oriental Room with its red China silk and antique blue china to the Cape Cod inspired Ocean Room, each one is different from the next.

Guests at the inn are welcome to use a communal refrigerator and microwave and coffee, iced tea, bottled water, and soft drinks are served throughout the day. In the morning, an expanded Continental breakfast is served with an array of items including flavored coffees, fresh juices, muffins and other baked items, breads, fresh fruit, and cereal.

"Greg and Candy, what an incredible place!
Your hospitality goes above and beyond the rest.
Thank you for all the laughs, for the wonderful breakfasts,
and the superb accommodations.
We will tell everyone to stop and stay!" — GUEST

INNKEEPERS:	Greg & Candy Grudovich
ADDRESS:	4931 SE Anchor Avenue, Stuart, Florida 34997
TELEPHONE:	(772) 286-6060
E-MAIL:	manateepocketinn@comcast.net
WEBSITE:	www.manateepocketinn.com
ROOMS:	5 Rooms; Private baths
CHILDREN:	Children age 8 and older welcome
PETS:	Not allowed

Peach & Blueberry Baked French Toast

Plan ahead, this dish needs to be refrigerated overnight!
Makes 8 Servings

"There are usually no leftovers after this breakfast — I even had a group tell me they were going to a brunch in a short time, but they couldn't resist having a piece anyway because it looked and smelled so good! This is a really wonderful dish to serve to vegetarians."

— INNKEEPER, *Manatee Pocket Inn*

1 can peach pie filling
1½ cups fresh or frozen blueberries
1 teaspoon ground cinnamon
7 eggs
1¾ cups milk
1 teaspoon vanilla extract
12 or 13 slices French bread, cubed
Maple syrup

Spray a 9x13-inch baking dish with non-stick cooking spray. Spread the peach pie filling evenly over the bottom and then sprinkle with the blueberries. In a large bowl, whisk together the cinnamon, eggs, milk, and vanilla. Immerse the bread cubes in the mixture and spoon over the fruit. Cover the dish and refrigerate overnight.

The following morning: Preheat oven to 375°F. Bake uncovered for 45 minutes, or until golden brown. Serve with maple syrup.

SEA BREEZE MANOR
B&B INN

In 1996, Lawrence and Patty Burke purchased this 1923 Tudor-style home and transformed it into a luxury beachside bed & breakfast. Both contractors by trade, the Burkes supervised every aspect of the renovation. As such, the home has been completely updated with every modern convenience, but still maintains its original charm. In 2002, after twenty years in D.C., Lori Rosso purchased the inn from the Burkes. A native of Long Island, Lori was thrilled to be running an inn on the beach and her years at the White House have made her a wonderful and hospitable host.

Sea Breeze is perfectly located between St. Petersburg and the Gulf of Mexico, overlooking the white sandy beaches and crystal clear waters of Boca Ciego Bay. Lori's goal is to provide her guests with luxurious and relaxing accommodations, a small piece of paradise that you will want to come back to again and again. Sea Breeze is all the comforts of home wrapped in a tropical and romantic setting.

INNKEEPER:	Lori Rosso
ADDRESS:	5701 Shore Boulevard South, Gulfport, Florida 33707
TELEPHONE:	(727) 343-4445; (888) 343-4445
E-MAIL:	rsvp@seabreezemanor.com
WEBSITE:	www.seabreezemanor.com
ROOMS:	4 Suites; 2 Cottages; Private & shared baths
CHILDREN:	Welcome
PETS:	Small dogs welcome; Call ahead

Easy, Elegant French Toast

Plan ahead, this dish needs to be refrigerated overnight!
Makes 6 Servings

"At first I only used berries in this dish, but then I branched out and found that peaches were an even better fit with the creaminess of the cream cheese. Frozen fruit works the best and should be thoroughly thawed in the microwave before using. Use regular cream cheese instead of the whipped variety. This recipe was adapted from one found in the St. Petersburg Area Association of B&B Inns Cookbook.*"*

— INNKEEPER, *Sea Breeze Manor*

1 loaf white bread
8 ounces cream cheese, cubed
1 (16 ounce) bag frozen peaches
10 eggs
1½ cups half & half
⅓ cup maple syrup
½ cup melted butter

Cut the bread into 1-inch cubes and spray a 9x13-inch baking dish with non-stick cooking spray. Place half of the bread cubes into the prepared dish; scatter with cream cheese pieces. Sprinkle the thawed peaches over the cream cheese and cover with the remaining bread cubes. In a large bowl, combine the eggs, half & half, syrup, and melted butter; mix well. Pour the egg mixture over the bread cubes. Cover the dish and refrigerate overnight.

The following morning: Preheat oven to 350°F. Bake uncovered for 40-50 minutes, or until set.

MANSION HOUSE
B&B INN & SPA

This traditional b&b in gorgeous St. Petersburg is conveniently located in the heart of the historic arts and entertainment district but is also just minutes from the new town center. The harbor, fine dining, shops, museums, and galleries are all just a few minutes' walk or drive away. Mornings at Mansion House begin with a full American breakfast that's made to order. Enjoy the inn's Jacuzzi and take advantage of the on-site spa. Head into town and visit the Florida Orange Groves and Winery then do some shopping at BayWalk. Treat yourself to a gourmet dinner at one of the many area restaurants and then return to the inn for the evening.

Each of the inn's twelve rooms has been individually decorated with your relaxation in mind. The following morning, take a dip in the inn's own pool and then head to the Dali Museum or Busch Gardens. Or, just spend the day reading a book under an umbrella at the beach.

INNKEEPERS:	Kathy & Peter Plautz & Diane Heron
ADDRESS:	105 5th Avenue NE, St. Petersburg, Florida 33701
TELEPHONE:	(727) 831-9391; (800) 274-7520
E-MAIL:	info@mansionhousebb.com
WEBSITE:	www.mansionbandb.com
ROOMS:	12 Rooms; Private baths
CHILDREN:	Children age 9 and older welcome
PETS:	Small dogs welcome

Peaches & Cream
Croissant French Toast

Plan ahead, this dish needs to be refrigerated overnight!
Makes 10 Servings

*"This recipe was a favorite of the innkeeper when we purchased the
inn three years ago. We have adopted it as our own "Mansion House"
recipe. This is great as a Sunday brunch or weekend dish,
but don't save it just for the weekend!"*
—INNKEEPER, *Mansion House B&B Inn & Spa*

½ cup sweet cream butter
1 cup brown sugar
2 tablespoons corn syrup
10 croissants, or French bread
1 bag frozen sliced peaches
1 (8 ounce) package cream cheese
1 dozen large eggs
1½ cups half & half
1 teaspoon vanilla extract

Grease a 9x13-inch pan. In a small saucepan over medium-high
heat, melt together the butter, brown sugar, and corn syrup; heat
until bubbly. Pour the mixture into the prepared pan and spread
the peaches over the top. Break the croissants into pieces and
place them on top of the peaches. Cut the cream cheese into little
pieces and scatter over the top of the croissants. In a blender, mix
the eggs, milk, and vanilla; pour over the croissants. Cover and
refrigerate the dish overnight.

The following morning: If you are using a glass dish, place the
dish into a cold oven and set to 350°F. If you are using any other
type of dish, preheat the oven. Bake the dish uncovered for
45 minutes. If the top begins to become too brown you can
cover with foil for the remaining cooking time. Serve with
Mansion House Yogurt Cream Sauce (a mixture of ½ yogurt,
½ whipped cream) and chopped pecans or hot maple syrup. For
a lighter dish, serve with sliced strawberries and powdered sugar.

Avera-Clarke House

This circa 1890 home was originally built and occupied by Florida state senator Thomas Clarke and his family. The house is a perfect example of Victorian architecture and is one of Monticello's famous historic homes. Now listed on the National Register of Historic Places, the Avera-Clarke house has been fully renovated and restored to its original splendor. Each tastefully appointed room features wood flooring, and period antique furnishings and décor.

Old Southern charm abounds at the Avera-Clarke House and innkeepers Gretchen and Troy are committed to providing guests with a stay like no other. Life's simple pleasures and warm hospitality are what you'll find here. Graceful oak and magnolia trees surround the property and whisper of days gone by. A stay at Monticello's Avera-Clarke House is perfect for some rest and relaxation away from the hustle and bustle of daily life.

INNKEEPERS: Gretchen & Troy Avera
ADDRESS: 580 West Washington Street, Monticello, Florida 32344
TELEPHONE: (850) 997-5007
E-MAIL: averaclarke@aol.com
WEBSITE: www.averaclarke.com
ROOMS: 5 Rooms; 1 Cottage; Private & shared baths
CHILDREN: Welcome
PETS: Small pets welcome; Resident pets

Peach French Toast

Plan ahead, this dish needs to refrigerate overnight!
Makes 8 Servings

"My return guests request this breakfast
when they make their reservations."
—INNKEEPER, *Avera-Clarke House*

4 large croissants
1 stick butter
1 cup packed browns sugar
2 tablespoons water
1 (29 ounce) can peaches,
     use fresh if available
6 eggs
1½ cups milk or cream
1 teaspoon vanilla extract

Tear the croissants into bite-sized pieces and set aside. In a medium saucepan over medium heat, stir together butter and brown sugar, heat until the butter is melted. Add the water and stir until the mixture bubbles; set aside to cool. Drain the peaches if using canned.

Spray a 9x13-inch baking dish with non-stick cooking spray. Pour in the cooled syrup mixture and layer the peaches into the dish. Cover with the croissant pieces – make sure you completely cover the peaches. In a medium bowl, mix together the eggs, milk or cream, and vanilla; pour over the bread. Push the bread down with your fingers to ensure that all of the liquid is soaked up. Cover and refrigerate overnight.

The following morning: Preheat oven to 350°F. Bake French toast for 40 minutes, or until the top is slightly browned. Slice and serve with fresh fruit, whipped cream, and warm syrup.

We serve this dish with smoked pork chops, bacon, or sausage.

MOUNT DORA HISTORIC INN

If comfort and tranquility are what you seek, Mount Dora is the place you'll find it. The Mount Dora Historic Inn whispers of time long ago and a much simpler life. Innkeepers Jim and Ana are gracious and hospitable hosts dedicated to providing guests with every comfort and amenity. The inn is truly a labor of love, and it shows in the warm and welcoming air.

The inn is a fully restored 1800s home located in downtown Mount Dora. Orlando is less than half an hour away, so you could easily take a day trip to the hottest tourist spots, or you could simply enjoy some time away from it all. Jim is a gourmet chef who is always busy with some new creation and Ana is always around to help you with anything that you might need.

INNKEEPERS: Jim & Ana Tuttle
ADDRESS: 221 East 4th Avenue, Mount Dora, Florida 32757
TELEPHONE: (352) 735-1212; (800) 927-6344
E-MAIL: innkeepermdhi@comcast.net
WEBSITE: www.mountdorahistoricinn.com
ROOMS: 4 Rooms; Private baths
CHILDREN: Welcome; Call ahead
PETS: Welcome; Call ahead

Chef Jim's Banana & Fuji Apple Stuffed French Toast

Plan ahead, this dish needs to be refrigerated overnight!
Makes 10-12 Servings

2 loaves French bread, not too crusty
8 ounces cream cheese, room temperature
4 ounces Ricotta cheese
2 ounces Mascarpone cheese
1 Fuji apple, cored and shredded
2 teaspoons cinnamon
$\frac{1}{3}$ cup brown sugar
Fresh ground nutmeg
3 bananas, mashed

cream mix:
2 large hen's eggs
2-2½ cups half & half
2 teaspoons vanilla extract

Slice the French bread to preference (we cut on a 2-inch bias, about a 45° angle), discard end pieces. Cut a slit in the top of each slice to create a pocket; set aside. In a large bowl, combine the three cheeses, apple, cinnamon, sugar, and nutmeg. Spoon the cheese/apple mixture into the bread pockets. Slice the bananas into ⅓-inch pieces and place one piece in each bread pocket. Set the bread pocket-side-up on a cookie sheet to prevent filling from spilling out. In a medium bowl, whisk together the cream ingredients. Roll each stuffed piece of bread in the mixture until well soaked. Place the bread, again pocket-side-up, on the cookie sheet, cover, and refrigerate overnight.

The following morning: Preheat an electric griddle to 300°F and the oven to 400°F. Coat the preheated griddle with non-stick cooking spray. Cook the French toast on the heated griddle, 3 minutes per side or until golden brown. Place browned pieces on a non-stick cookie sheet and bake in the oven for an additional 5-6 minutes, turning over after 3 minutes. Serve with a dusting of powdered sugar, bacon or kielbasa, maple syrup, and butter.

Herlong Mansion
Historic Inn & Gardens

The elegant and stately Herlong Mansion in historic Micanopy was built in 1845. Originally, the home was a "cracker style" farm home with a detached kitchen. Natalie Herlong, nee Simonton, came into possession of the home and worked with her husband to transform it into a Greek revival mansion. In 1910, the structure was covered in a brick imitation of the Southern colonial home complete with four Corinthian-style columns. Inside the home features classic arts and crafts-style leaded glass windows,

wood paneling, and intricate oak, maple, and mahogany flooring.

Deemed by *Florida Trend Magazine* to be "easily Florida's most elegant B&B," this popular bed & breakfast now has six guest rooms, three suites, and three cottages. Each room features beautiful and stylish antiques and furnishings. In true Southern style, the inn's wide verandas sport rocking chairs and cushioned swings great for a lazy afternoon overlooking the lush gardens and picturesque landscape. Herlong is the perfect place for a quiet and leisurely vacation, a treat and respite from the busy everyday grind.

INNKEEPERS: Carolyn & Stephen West

ADDRESS: 402 NE Cholokka Blvd, Micanopy, Florida 32667

TELEPHONE: (352) 466-3322; (800) 437-5664

E-MAIL: info@herlong.com

WEBSITE: www.herlong.com

ROOMS: 12 Rooms; 2 Suites; 2 Cottages; Private baths

CHILDREN: Welcome

PETS: Small pets welcome; Call ahead

Pear Crème Brûlée "French Toast"

Plan ahead, this dish needs to be refrigerated overnight!
Makes 10-12 Servings

"Our wild pear tree presented so many pears that we created this special breakfast dish so that our guests could share our bounty."

—INNKEEPER, *Herlong Mansion*

1 stick unsalted butter
1 cup brown sugar
2 tablespoons corn syrup
Chopped pecans
6 medium pears, cored and sliced
6 large (or 12 mini) croissants, cubed
6 eggs
1½ cups half & half
1 (8 ounce) block cream cheese, cubed
1 teaspoon vanilla extract
1 teaspoon Grand Marnier (or orange extract)
¼ teaspoon salt
Crème Anglaise, for serving

In a medium saucepan over medium heat, melt the butter with the brown sugar and corn syrup; stir until smooth and pour into a greased 13x9-inch baking pan. Sprinkle the chopped pecans over the butter mixture and top with a layer of sliced pears. Evenly distribute the cubed croissants over the sliced pear layer and top with the cream cheese. In a medium bowl, whisk together the eggs, half & half, Grand Marnier, and salt and pour the mixture over the casserole. Cover and chill 8 hours or overnight.

The following morning: Bring the dish to room temperature. Preheat oven to 350°F and bake 40 minutes.

To serve: Cut into squares and plate with the pears on top. Pour Crème Anglaise over the top and serve.

Sunset Bay Inn

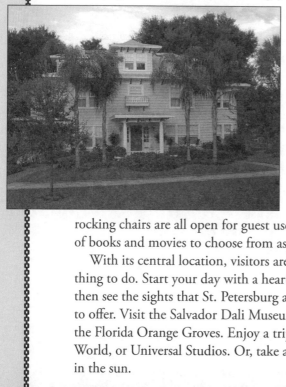

Enjoy old-world charm and modern amenities at the Sunset Bay Inn. This circa 1911 home is located in the quiet historic northeast neighborhood of St. Petersburg, just a five minute walk from downtown. Guests call the inn a "surprising pearl" and the enchanting and hospitable Linda a "wonderful host who can cook!"

The inn has a total of eight guest rooms, three of which are suites. Each room has a unique design with floral accents. The antique filled living room, sunroom, and veranda complete with rocking chairs are all open for guest use and there are a wide variety of books and movies to choose from as well.

With its central location, visitors are sure to always find something to do. Start your day with a hearty and filling breakfast and then see the sights that St. Petersburg and the surrounding area have to offer. Visit the Salvador Dali Museum, The Pier Aquarium, or the Florida Orange Groves. Enjoy a trip to Busch Gardens, Disney World, or Universal Studios. Or, take a book to the beach and relax in the sun.

INNKEEPER: Linda Collette

ADDRESS: 635 Bay Street NE, St. Petersburg, Florida 33701

TELEPHONE: (727) 896-6701; (800) 794-5133

E-MAIL: innkeeper@sunsetbayinn.com

WEBSITE: www.sunsetbayinn.com

ROOMS: 8 Rooms; 3 Suites; Private baths

CHILDREN: Children age 8 and older welcome

PETS: Small dogs allowed

BANANA FRENCH TOAST

Makes 4 Servings

8 slices raisin bread
2 medium bananas, sliced
1 cup milk
4 ounces cream cheese, softened
3 eggs
$\frac{1}{3}$ cup sugar
3 tablespoons flour
2 teaspoons vanilla extract

Preheat oven to 350°F. Place four slices of raisin bread in a buttered or greased 9x9-inch baking dish. Top with the sliced bananas and the remaining 4 slices of raisin bread. Using a food processor or a blender, combine the milk, cream cheese, eggs, sugar, flour, and vanilla. Blend until smooth. Pour the mixture over the raisin bread and let stand 5 minutes (you could also cover the dish and refrigerate it overnight at this point). Bake 40-45 minutes, until set and the top is toasted. Let stand 10 minutes before slicing into diagonals and plating.

Dust with powdered sugar and garnish with fruit to serve.

Puffy Apple Pancake

Makes 6 Servings

3 eggs, separated
2 tablespoons sugar
½ cup half & half
⅓ cup pancake mix
2 tablespoons orange juice
¼ teaspoon cinnamon
1 small nutmeg, grated
1 large apple, peeled and thinly sliced

Topping:
1 tablespoon sugar
½ teaspoon cinnamon
¼ cup chopped walnuts

Preheat oven to 375°F. Grease a 9-inch pie plate and place it in the heating oven until you are ready to use. In a medium bowl, beat the egg whites until they are firm, gradually adding the sugar until stiff peaks form; set aside. In a separate bowl, combine the egg yolks, pancake mix, half & half, orange juice, cinnamon, and nutmeg. Mix until blended. Gently fold the egg whites into the pancake batter and spoon into the hot pie plate. Top with the apple slices and sprinkle with topping. Bake 15 minutes, until puffy and golden. Drizzle with maple syrup and powdered sugar; serve with fruit.

For the topping: In a small bowl, mix together all the topping ingredients making sure that the cinnamon and walnuts are evenly distributed in the mixture.

PANCAKES have been featured in cookbooks as far back as 1439. They are enjoyed in almost every country, but have slight variations:

German and French pancakes are baked very thin and served with both sweet and savory fillings.

The Old English mixed ale, or beer, into their pancake batter.

Russian blinis use buckwheat and are served with caviar and sour cream.

The Irish make their pancakes with soda-water and buttermilk.

In New Zealand they're called pikelets and are served with jam and cream or butter.

In the Netherlands, they call their pancakes pannenkoeken and they eat them at dinner.

St. Francis Inn

Breakfast at the St. Francis Inn is a true event. Each morning guests are treated to a fabulous collection of mouthwatering creations courtesy of Chef Gary Douylliez and his kitchen staff. Items like the Cinnamon Pecan French Toast, Citrus Pancakes with Mandarin Orange Sauce, and Biscuits with Sausage Gravy are just a few of the ever-changing daily menus. Afternoons, guests can mingle at the daily Social Hour and enjoy complimentary beverages, antipasto, Parmesan Artichoke Dip, and a host of other hors d'oeuvres. As if that weren't enough, the St. Francis also has an evening dessert selection. Homemade dessert delicacies, coffee, hot chocolate, and assorted teas are served from 7:30-9:00 p.m.

"My husband and I just returned from a three night stay at The St. Francis Inn. It was a wonderful experience! The property itself is lovely and historic, but modern comforts abound. Our Jacuzzi bathtub (in the Overlook Room) was definitely appreciated by this stressed out mom! [We] also enjoyed an afternoon by the swimming pool and it was just the two of us. Every day, the hot breakfast buffet was delicious, as was the sherry that came complimentary with our room… [but] all of these things cannot compare to the wonderful staff! We will definitely be returning to this gem in St. Augustine!" —GUEST

INNKEEPERS: Joe & Margaret Finnegan

ADDRESS: 279 St. George Street, St. Augustine, Florida 32084

TELEPHONE: (904) 824-6068; (800) 824-6062

E-MAIL: innkeeper@stfrancisinn.com

WEBSITE: www.stfrancisinn.com

ROOMS: 12 Rooms; 4 Suites; 1 Cottage; Private baths

CHILDREN: Call ahead

PETS: Small pets welcome; Call ahead; Resident pets

Luau Custard French Toast

Plan ahead, this dish needs to refrigerate at least 1 hour, or overnight!
Makes 6-8 Servings

1 loaf French bread
10 large eggs, beaten
2 cups milk
1 (13.5 ounce) can coconut milk
1 tablespoon vanilla extract
¾ cup brown sugar
1 (15 ounce) can pineapple tidbits,
    drained and juice reserved
1½ cups flaked coconut

Luau Maple Syrup:
1 pound brown sugar
1 (13.5) ounce coconut milk
1 cup maple syrup
1 teaspoon vanilla extract
Reserved pineapple juice

For the French toast: Spray a 13x9-inch casserole dish with non-stick cooking spray. Slice the bread into 1-inch slices and place in the bottom of the dish. In a large bowl, combine the eggs, milk, coconut milk, vanilla extract, and brown sugar. Pour the custard mixture over the bread slices and top with pineapple bits and flaked coconut. Cover and refrigerate at least 1 hour or overnight.

To bake: Remove the dish from the refrigerator and preheat oven to 350°F. Bake uncovered for 45 minutes, or until center is set. Serve with Luau Maple Syrup.

For the syrup: While your French toast is baking, combine all of the syrup ingredients together in a medium saucepan. Bring the mixture to a boil and simmer 5 minutes. Serve warm.

Sunshine State
Stuffed French Toast

Plan ahead, this dish needs to refrigerate at least one hour or up to overnight!

Makes 8-10 Servings

1 loaf Italian bread
8 ounces cream cheese, softened
1 cup orange marmalade
10 eggs
1 cup milk
1 cup orange juice
¾ cup brown sugar

Slice the bread into 2-inch slices and cut a pocket ¾ of the way through each slice. Spread each side of the interior pocket with cream cheese and fill with 1 tablespoon of orange marmalade. Spray a 13x9-inch baking dish with non-stick cooking spray and place the stuffed slices into the dish. In a large bowl, mix together the eggs, milk, and orange juice. Pour the mixture over the stuffed slices, cover and refrigerate at least one hour or up to overnight.

To bake: Remove the dish from the refrigerator, uncover, and preheat oven to 350°F. Sprinkle the brown sugar over the top of the stuffed slices and bake 30-35 minutes.

Citrus Pancakes with Mandarin Orange Sauce

Makes 4-6 Servings

Pancakes:
2 cups Buttermilk Pancake Mix
1½ cups orange juice
¼ cup warm water
Zest from 1 orange

Mandarin Orange Sauce:
1 (15 ounce) can Mandarin orange slices in light syrup
2 teaspoons sugar
½ teaspoon vanilla extract
¼ cup cold water
1 tablespoon cornstarch
1 tablespoon frozen concentrated orange juice

For the pancakes: In a medium bowl, whisk together the pancake mix, orange juice, water, and orange zest. Drop by spoonfuls onto a heated griddle. Flip when bubbles begin to break. Remove and plate when the bottom has browned and the pancakes have puffed.

For the orange sauce: In a medium saucepan, heat the oranges, juice, sugar, and vanilla over medium-high heat. In a small bowl, stir together the cornstarch and water. When the orange mixture comes to a boil, stir in the cornstarch mixture. Cook stirring constantly until the sauce has thickened.

To serve: Plate the pancakes in desired portions and top with warm Mandarin Orange Sauce.

HENDERSON PARK INN

The Henderson Park Inn is Destin's own all-inclusive, adults-only, romantic beach resort. Each of the spacious 32 guest suites features Victorian-style furnishing and luxurious linens, and most have whirlpool tubs and their very own private balcony. On the night of your arrival, you'll find grapes, wine, and flowers waiting for you in your suite. The following morning, you'll enjoy a hearty Southern-style breakfast. For lunch, Henderson Park supplies all of its guests with gourmet boxed lunches featuring items like honey-pecan chicken salad and wild salmon sandwiches, perfect for a picnic on the beach.

Spend your afternoon lounging on the beach and take advantage of the inn's beachside service. Beach chairs, umbrellas, and towels are provided and complimentary water bottles, soft drinks, and candy bars are available all day long. At sunset, you'll enjoy a wine and beer hour out on the inn's sundeck. The proximity to Henderson Park, a 208 acre state park, and the adults-only setting make this a peaceful and romantic place for anyone, whether you're celebrating an anniversary, planning a wedding, or simply looking for a quiet weekend away.

INNKEEPER:	Ryan Olin
ADDRESS:	2700 Scenic Hwy 98 E, Destin, Florida 32541
TELEPHONE:	(850) 269-8646; (866) 398-4432
E-MAIL:	rolin@hendersonparkinn.com
WEBSITE:	www.hendersonparkinn.com
ROOMS:	32 Suites; Private baths
CHILDREN:	Cannot accommodate
PETS:	Not allowed

Pecan Pancakes

Makes 6-8 Servings

1½ cups all-purpose flour
3½ teaspoons baking powder
1 teaspoon salt
1 tablespoon sugar
1¼ cups milk
1 egg
3 tablespoons melted butter
½ cup chopped pecans

In a large bowl, sift together the flour, baking powder, salt, and sugar. Make a well in the center of the mixture and pour in the milk, egg, and melted butter; mix until smooth. Fold in the pecans.

Heat a lightly oiled griddle or frying pan over medium-high heat. Pour ¼ cup of batter into the pan and brown on both sides. Repeat until all of the batter has been used.

Serve with pure maple syrup, fresh whipped cream, and additional pecans for garnish.

Casa Thorn

Let Thorn Trainer and her wonderful staff at Casa Thorn make your next vacation one that you'll always remember. Their dedication to providing great service and their attention to every detail ensures that you will never want for anything as long as you are there. From the gourmet breakfast and the dinner suggestions to the tropical paradise atmosphere, this is one b&b experience that shouldn't be missed.

"My husband and I stayed at [Casa] Thorn earlier this month. It was an absolutely wonderful experience. [The] rooms are all quite private and very tastefully decorated. Thorn is very conscious of the up-keep of her place [and it] really shows. She makes herself available for questions, but is also respectful of your privacy. Her assistants, Mary Ann and Cindy, were joyful and eager to make our stay a pleasant one. They too, went out of their way to provide a private and comfortable atmosphere with the perfect personal touch. A fabulous breakfast was served on our private porch each morning. I can't say enough about Casa Thorn and the people who run it..." —GUEST

INNKEEPERS: Thorn Trainer, Cindy Dobbs, & Mary Ann Nichols
ADDRESS: 114 Palm Lane, Islamorada, Florida 33036
TELEPHONE: (305) 852-3996
E-MAIL: casathorn@webtv.net
WEBSITE: www.casathorn.com
ROOMS: 5 Rooms; Private & shared baths
CHILDREN: Children age 8 and older welcome
PETS: Small pets welcome; Resident pets

Banana Pecan Pancakes

Makes 4 Servings (8 Pancakes)

"The previous staff at Casa Thorn served a banana pancake dish that returning guests asked us to prepare. We'd never made them before but thought we'd give them a try. Then we found out that early in Thorn's career, she had been in a television commercial that parodied the "Chiquita Banana Girls." We knew we had to find a recipe. We called on Cindy's mom and she sent us this recipe as well as another. Her tip is to make sure the griddle is hot before pouring the batter. This will get you perfectly golden pancakes."

—INNKEEPER, *Casa Thorn*

1 cup pancake mix (just-add-water variety)
$^2/_3$ cup water
1 small banana, peeled and mashed
2 tablespoons finely chopped pecans

In a medium mixing bowl, combine the pancake mix and water. Stir in the mashed bananas and pecans.

Spray a non-stick griddle with non-stick cooking spray and allow to heat before pouring in your pancake batter. Ladle pancake batter onto the heated griddle and cook until the edges of the pancake are dry; turn over and cook until the other side is firm. Remove pancakes to a serving platter and serve immediately.

The Cottage B&B

Join the ranks of such splendid guests as Kirstie Alley and Shalim Ortiz (*Heroes*) in enjoying all that The Cottage B&B has to offer. A luxurious and peaceful escape from the daily grind located in beautiful Monticello, this inn is the result of years of loving effort. The results are clear in the five-star accommodations. Spend the weekend with that special someone and enjoy a romantic getaway that you'll never forget. The inn has just two guest rooms, which means that you'll enjoy privacy and the pampering attentions of your innkeepers, Jean Michel and Martha. Each of the rooms is

unique and features crisp linens, fine art, garden views, cozy robes, and a mini-fridge.

While the surrounding area offers plenty of shopping and fine-dining options, guests can arrange for luncheons and romantic candle-lit dinners courtesy of the inn. You can choose from a variety of menu options such as ancho chili-seared steak, jerk-maple salmon, and the famous house pasta with chicken breast and tarragon, cream, cognac sauce. Dinner is a full-course event from salad to dessert and even a complimentary glass of wine.

The Cottage B&B is also a great place to have a wedding. The Venetian Garden is elegant and romantic, and perfect for small get-togethers. The inn will even host your wedding weekend complete with catering.

INNKEEPERS: Jean Michel & Martha Cravanzola

ADDRESS: 295 West Palmer Mill Road, Monticello, Florida 32344

TELEPHONE: (850) 342-3541; (866) 342-3541

E-MAIL: mjmbandb@yahoo.com

WEBSITE: www.thecottagebedbreakfastandrestaurant.4t.com

ROOMS: 2 Rooms; Private baths

CHILDREN: Children age 8 and older welcome

PETS: Not allowed; Resident pets

Banana & Peanut Butter Pancakes

Makes 3-4 Servings

"You can call these 'Elvis Specials' if served with honey and bacon!"
—INNKEEPER, *The Cottage Bed & Breakfast*

1¼ cups flour
2½ teaspoons baking powder
½ teaspoon salt
1¼ cups milk
1 egg
¼ cup peanut butter, smooth or chunky
1 banana
3 tablespoons melted butter
3 tablespoons honey

In a small bowl, sift together the flour, baking powder, and salt. In a medium bowl, whisk together the milk, egg, and melted butter. In a food processor, purée the banana and blend with the peanut butter. Add the banana/peanut butter mixture, the melted butter, and honey to the egg mixture and mix to combine. Stir in the dry ingredients until just moistened. Allow the mixture to sit 15 minutes before cooking.

Pour a ¼ cup of the batter onto a hot griddle or skillet and cook until bubbles form around the edges. Flip and cook until golden brown. Repeat until all the batter has been used.

Tips and Variations

Try using half of a slightly green banana and half of a very ripe banana for great flavor and texture.

OUR HOUSE OF ST. AUGUSTINE

Our House is actually two neighboring 1880s Victorian homes. Owner Dave Brezing purchased the first home in 2001 and fully restored it to its historic elegance. Then, in 2005, he expanded Our House and added the garden suites. Elegant heart-pine floors and carefully chosen period antiques grace every inch of this lovely inn. Dave's luxurious romantic retreat, a true home-away-from-home, is set in a quiet residential area of St. Augustine, just a short walk from all the historic tourist attractions, shopping, and dining of the main drag.

Let yourself relax and enjoy the warmth of Our House before you venture into town. Each morning you'll awaken to the sounds of the 1923 Chickering grand piano summoning you to a hearty three-course breakfast. Coffee service is delivered right to your room or, for studio guests, you'll find everything you need in your own kitchenette. Dave is an experienced traveler who has stayed in dozens of b&bs himself and his own experience has proved to be great research for the inn. His attention to every detail is obvious and his goal is to make guests feel right at home.

INNKEEPER: Dave Brezing

ADDRESS: 7 Cincinnati Avenue, St. Augustine, Florida 32084

TELEPHONE: (904) 347-6260

E-MAIL: ourhouse@ourhouseofstaugustine.com

WEBSITE: www.ourhouseofstaugustine.com

ROOMS: 5 Rooms; Private baths

CHILDREN: Children age 14 and older welcome

PETS: Not allowed

Sweet Potato Pancakes

Makes 4-6 Servings

*"Try substituting mashed pumpkin instead of sweet potatoes
and garnish with cranberry jam for a fun fall twist."*
—INNKEEPER, *Our House of St. Augustine*

1½ cups unbleached all-purpose flour
1 teaspoon sugar
$\frac{1}{8}$ teaspoon salt
½ teaspoon pumpkin pie spice
1½ teaspoons baking powder
1 teaspoon baking soda
1 tablespoon melted butter
1 large egg
1½ cups buttermilk
1 heaping cup cooked,
    mashed sweet potatoes (canned is fine)

In a large bowl, sift together the flour, sugar, salt, pumpkin pie spice, baking powder, and baking soda. In a separate bowl, mix together the melted butter, egg, buttermilk, and mashed sweet potato. Pour the wet mixture into the bowl with the flour mixture and mix well to fully combine, adding additional buttermilk if necessary. Mixture will be the texture of a thick, lumpy milkshake – do not over mix, lumps are ok.

Heat a large skillet or griddle over medium-high heat. Ladle about ¼ cup of the batter onto the griddle. When bubbles begin to appear on the surface of the pancake, flip it over and cook until golden brown. Repeat until all of the batter has been used.

Captains' Inn

The Captains' Inn in historic Mount Dora is a great place for family vacations and romantic getaways. Each guest is treated like one of the family at this tropical inn. Captains Barry and Tamara Spieler have twenty-five years of experience running charter yachts and mega-yachts. Some of their clientele has included heads

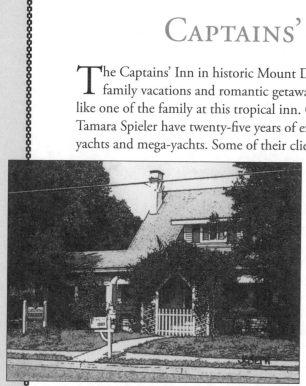

of state, movie stars, and of course, the rich and famous. They now bring their combined experience in the hospitality industry to their unique nautical themed bed & breakfast.

Tamara is a world-class chef who serves up her wonderful creations each morning at breakfast. You can also book a private candlelight dinner or an outdoor barbecue. The inn has multiple outdoor dining options including a covered bar and grill area.

The Captains' Inn also offers chartered fishing trips. Captain Barry will regale you with tales of his time at sea as he guides you to the best local fishing spots aboard the inn's own *Mount Dorable*.

INNKEEPERS: Captains Barry & Tamara Spieler
ADDRESS: 1507 North Donnelly Street, Mount Dora, Florida 32757
TELEPHONE: (352) 383-0650
E-MAIL: tnbcaptains@aol.com
WEBSITE: www.captainsinnmountdora.com
ROOMS: 3 Rooms; 1 Suite; Private baths
CHILDREN: Welcome
PETS: Dogs welcome; Resident pet

Apple Puffed Pancakes

Makes 6 Servings

*"My sister-in-law, Marsha, gave me this recipe,
and every time I serve it, the comment is, "Wonderful!"*
—INNKEEPER, Captains' Inn

6 eggs
1½ cups milk
1 cup flour
3 tablespoons sugar
1 teaspoon vanilla extract
¼ teaspoon cinnamon
½ teaspoon salt
¼ pound butter
2 apples, peeled and thinly sliced
3 tablespoons light brown sugar

Preheat oven to 375°F. In a blender, mix together the eggs, milk, flour, sugar, vanilla, cinnamon, and salt until blended. Melt the butter in a 12-inch fluted quiche dish; remove from oven and add in a single layer of apple slices. Pour the batter over the apples and sprinkle with the brown sugar.

Bake 45-60 minutes and serve immediately with warm maple syrup.

Gingerbread Waffles
with Strawberries

Makes 6 Servings

"This recipe is featured in my cookbook, Mega Yacht Cooking.*"*

—*INNKEEPER, Captains' Inn*

1½ cups heavy cream
5 eggs, separated, yolks beaten
¾ cup light molasses
1 cup dark brown sugar
2⅔ cups flour
6 teaspoons baking powder
¾ teaspoon cinnamon
2 teaspoons ground ginger
1 teaspoon allspice
½ teaspoon ground cloves
¾ pound butter, melted
½ pound strawberries, sliced

In a large bowl, using an electric mixer, combine the cream, egg yolks, molasses, and brown sugar. In a separate bowl, sift together the flour, baking powder, cinnamon, ginger, allspice, and cloves. Add the butter and the flour mixture to the cream mixture, mixing until combined. In a separate bowl, beat the egg whites until fluffy and fold into the batter. Bake mixture in a waffle iron.

Top waffles with sliced strawberries and serve with hot maple syrup.

Banana Kiwi Crêpes

Makes 8 Servings

"This recipe is taken from my own cookbooks, Ships' Bounty.*"*
—*INNKEEPER, Captains' Inn*

2 eggs
½ cup coconut milk
¼ cup milk
1 cup flour
1 tablespoon sugar
1 tablespoon butter, melted
Oil for frying
Powdered sugar for dusting
Salt

Filling:
3 tablespoons butter
3 tablespoons light brown sugar
4 bananas, sliced
4 kiwis, sliced
½ cup orange juice
3 tablespoons dark rum

For the crêpes: In a bowl, whisk together the eggs, coconut milk, and milk. In a separate mixing bowl, sift together the flour and salt; stir in sugar. Gradually beat in the egg mixture to form a smooth batter; stir in melted butter.

Heat an 8-inch non-stick skillet and brush with a little oil. Pour in enough batter to just coat the base of the pan – tip the pan so that batter distributes evenly. Cook until the bottom is browned, flip over and cook the other side. Remove from pan and keep warm while cooking remaining crêpes.

For the filling: Melt the butter in a skillet and stir in the sugar. Add the bananas and kiwis and sauté until the fruit softens. Add the orange juice and the rum; boil rapidly until the liquid is reduced and thickened.

To serve: Place a spoonful of filling on one quarter of each crêpe. Fold the crêpes in half over the filling and then once again into quarters. Dust with powdered sugar and serve hot.

Harrington House
Beachfront
Bed & Breakfast

As one of Florida's most highly rated b&bs, Harrington House is dedicated to providing top-quality service and extraordinary accommodations. Bask in the sounds of the ocean and take in the astonishing views. Experience the charm and genuine hospitality of this beach paradise.

Harrington House is not one, but four buildings located right on Holmes Beach. The inn consists of a main house, the Carriage House, the Dodt House, and the Huth Beach House. The main inn, built in 1925 houses eight of the inn's guest rooms. Breakfast at the Harrington House is served daily in the main inn. The Carriage House was built in the 1940s and has five suites to choose from. The Dodt House, named for Dr. Dodt, was built in the 1930s and has three suites, great for extra-long stays. Finally, the Huth Beach House was built in the 1960s and was home to one of Anna Maria Island's first doctors. The house has four different suites and a wonderful view of the gulf. In addition to the inn's main buildings, they have also recently added two bungalows for rental. These are perfect for visiting families on extended vacation.

INNKEEPERS: Patti & Mark Davis

ADDRESS: 5626 Gulf Drive, Holmes Beach, Florida 34217

TELEPHONE: (941) 778-5444; (888) 828-5566

E-MAIL: fbbi@harringtonhouse.com

WEBSITE: www.harringtonhouse.com

ROOMS: 20 Rooms; Private baths

CHILDREN: Children age 12 and older welcome

PETS: Not allowed

Crêpes with Spiced Orange Compote

Makes 30 Crêpes and 3 Quarts Compote

*"This sauce was originally used as a duck sauce
at an up-state New York steak/seafood house."*
—INNKEEPER, *Harrington House Beachfront B&B*

Crêpes:
2 tablespoons sugar
2 cups flour
6 eggs
7 teaspoons melted butter
1⅓ cups milk
½ teaspoon salt
¼ teaspoon nutmeg

Spiced Orange Compote:
½ gallon plus ½ cup orange juice
½ pound light brown sugar
1 teaspoon ground cinnamon
1 teaspoon ground nutmeg
1 teaspoon allspice
1 teaspoon cloves
¼ cup cornstarch
4 cups orange segments

Toasted macadamia nuts, crushed, for garnish

For the crêpes: Combine all ingredients, mixing until well incorporated. Cover and refrigerate, allowing the batter 24 hours to rest. When ready to cook, heat a non-stick skillet over medium heat and pour 1 ounce of the batter into the pan. Cook until golden brown on both sides. Repeat until all of the batter has been used, cool the crêpes before serving.

For the compote: In a 2-gallon stock-pot, combine the ½ gallon of orange juice with the brown sugar and spices. Bring the mixture to a boil and reduce to a simmer. In a separate bowl, combine the ½ cup orange juice with the cornstarch. Add the cornstarch slurry to the simmering orange stock, enough to thicken to a sauce consistency. Add the orange segments to the pot and keep over a low heat making sure not to break up the orange segments.

To serve: Top the crêpes with a generous portion of the compote and top with crushed, toasted macadamia nuts.

Egg & Breakfast Entrées

Egg & Breakfast Entrées

> " An egg is always an adventure;
>
> the next one may be different. "
>
> —OSCAR WILDE

ADDISON ON AMELIA

If you're looking for a peaceful and relaxing stay at the beach, the Addison on Amelia is the perfect place for you. Each of the inn's fourteen guest rooms feature hardwood floors, luxury linens, and jetted tubs or spa quality showers and a private or semi-private

porch overlooking Ash Street or the inn's central courtyard. Each evening guests are invited to join innkeepers Shannon and Bob for a happy hour with wine, beer, and hors d'oeuvres. A mouthwatering and hearty breakfast is included with every stay. Though the selection changes daily, you're always in for a treat with items such as the inn's signature smoothies, breakfast in a boat, banana pancakes with pecan toffee syrup, and breakfast quesadillas. For coffee lovers, the inn also serves organic Peruvian fair trade coffee, available at any time of day.

Just a short walk finds you amongst Amelia Island's Historic District shopping and dining and Bob and Shannon will gladly make suggestions and recommendations to guests. A host of other activities are also available on the island including sailing and kayaking, historic and eco tours, golf, and horseback riding. You can also lounge on the beach and make use of the inn's complimentary beach towels and umbrellas.

INNKEEPERS: Shannon & Bob Tidball

ADDRESS: 614 Ash Street, Fernandina Beach, Florida 32034

TELEPHONE: (904) 277-1604; (800) 943-1604

E-MAIL: info@addisononamelia.com

WEBSITE: www.addisononamelia.com

ROOMS: 14 Rooms; Private baths

CHILDREN: Children age 14 and older welcome

PETS: Not allowed; Resident pet

Addison's Breakfast in a Boat

Makes 4 Servings

"On a pleasant morning, Ben, Shannon, Lee, and Grant were enjoying the Addison's courtyard fountain and brainstorming ideas for breakfast when the breakfast boat was born. The boat was a great way to use eggs and potatoes in an unpredictable way. We're still trying to come up with more nautical ideas for the boat, and so are our guests – one fashioned oars out of the orange rind from his garnish!"
—INNKEEPER, *Addison on Amelia*

2 large baking potatoes
¼ cup vegetable oil
Coarse kosher salt
4 strips bacon
8 extra large eggs
1 cup shredded Mexican four-cheese blend

Preheat oven to 425°F. Scrub the potatoes and coat them with oil. Sprinkle all sides with kosher salt and bake until tender, about 1 hour. Allow the potatoes to cool completely before cutting in half lengthwise. Hollow the potatoes with a spoon, leaving about ¼-inch thick potato skin shell – this will be your boat.

Cook the bacon until it is crisp; chop into small bits and set aside. Scramble the eggs in a large, non-stick skillet until they are almost done but still slightly sloppy. Place the potato boats on a microwave-safe plate and spoon an equal amount of the scrambled eggs into each. Sprinkle with shredded cheese and heat in the microwave 45 seconds to 1 minute, or until the cheese is melted (this step will also finish cooking the eggs). Use tongs to place each boat onto a serving plate and top with the chopped bacon bits. Serve with hash browns.

Tips and Variations

The potato skin shells may be refrigerated overnight and then warmed in a low oven while preparing the rest of the dish. The scooped out centers can be used for making hash browns.

CAPTAINS' INN

The nautical themed Captains' Inn in Mount Dora has truly unique and amazing accommodations. Originally built in 1925 and completely renovated in 2007, the inn features four "staterooms" each named for a famous film captain. The Captain Jack Sparrow suite is decorated in a ruby red and gold theme and even has *Pirates of the Caribbean* photos and decorative pieces. The Captain Hook stateroom has its own private entrance and patio area. The other two rooms are named for Captain Morgan Adams of Cutthroat Island and Captain Ahab. This is a great family vacation retreat. Each room either has extra space for kids, or in the case of the Captain Ahab stateroom, can be converted as an extra room for kids.

The Captains' Inn has an outdoor heated pool and Jacuzzi. They also have a number of common areas that are perfect for relaxing and hanging out with the family. The outdoor cabana looks out on the pool and has plenty of lounging area as well as a pool table and entertainment center. There's an outdoor seating area with fireplace and even a wedding gazebo where Captain Barry, a licensed Captain and minister can perform your service complete with maritime vows. The outdoor fountain game lounge and the library also provide hours of entertainment options for guests who want to spend their day at the inn. Captains' Inn is also conveniently located just a short drive from some of Florida's most popular tourist destinations. The Captains' Inn truly has something for everyone whether you're looking for a great wedding and honeymoon destination, a nice family getaway, or just a relaxing weekend away from it all.

INNKEEPERS: Captains Barry & Tamara Spieler

ADDRESS: 1507 North Donnelly Street, Mount Dora, Florida 32757

TELEPHONE: (352) 383-0650

E-MAIL: tnbcaptains@aol.com

WEBSITE: www.captainsinnmountdora.com

ROOMS: 3 Rooms; 1 Suite; Private baths

CHILDREN: Welcome

PETS: Dogs welcome; Resident pet

Baked Eggs with Bacon

Makes 6 Servings

"This recipe comes from my own cookbook, Mega Yacht Cooking, *and is an adaptation of the ever popular Eggs Benedict."*
—INNKEEPER, *Captains' Inn*

12 eggs
12 slices cooked bacon
1 can sliced pineapple, slices halved
6 teaspoons butter, melted
3 tablespoons chives, chopped
12 English muffins, halved
¼ pound blue cheese, crumbled
Cooking spray
Butter for English muffins
Assorted fruit, for serving

Preheat oven to 350°F. Spray a 12-cup non-stick muffin pan with cooking spray. Place ½ teaspoon melted butter into each muffin cup and top with half of a slice of pineapple. Wrap one slice of bacon around the inside rim of each cup. Break one egg into each cup and top with chives and blue cheese. Bake 12 minutes.

Carefully remove eggs from muffin cups and place on buttered English muffin halves. Garnish with assorted fruits and serve.

SoBeYou B&B

In the heart of popular South Beach lies the SoBeYou, an intimate and tropical oasis with ten poolside guest rooms and suites. Each room features elegant Art Deco style décor and luxury bedding. SoBeYou is a haven for guests who desire peace and privacy. It's also centrally located so you are always just a few short steps from the beach, fine dining, shops, and other South Beach attractions.

Breakfast at this inn is not to be missed. Each morning guest will be treated to a variety of homemade items like multigrain walnut pancakes and shirred eggs with tarragon mornay sauce. This hearty and mouthwatering meal is served poolside amongst the lush garden and palm trees. The inn's friendly staff are dedicated to providing exemplary service and making sure that you, the guest, are always the center of attention.

INNKEEPER: Susan Culligan

ADDRESS: 1018 Jefferson Avenue, Miami Beach, Florida 33139

TELEPHONE: (305) 534-5247; (877) 599-5247

E-MAIL: info@sobeyou.us

WEBSITE: www.sobeyou.us

ROOMS: 10 Rooms; Private & shared baths

CHILDREN: Children age 1 and older welcome

PETS: Welcome

French Swiss Melt

Makes 6 Servings

*"When Susan, the owner, bought Bradford Gardens,
a world renowned bed & breakfast in Provincetown, Massachusetts,
the former owner gave her six recipes. Susan had to
come up with a seventh on her own and that is how
she created this mouthwatering dish."*

—INNKEEPER, *SoBeYou Bed & Breakfast*

6 eggs
1½ cups milk
3 tablespoons cinnamon
6 English muffins
1½ cups Swiss cheese
½ cup walnuts
3 cups low-fat vanilla yogurt
4 cups fresh cut fruit of choice*
12 diced strawberries
Fresh mint sprigs, for garnish
Maple syrup, to serve

In a medium bowl, mix together the eggs, milk, and cinnamon. Cut the English muffins in half and dip them in the mixture until they are fully moistened. Spread a skillet or griddle with "all vegetable" shortening. Cook the muffins over high heat for 2 minutes, lower the heat and turn the muffins over to cook an additional 1½ minutes. Place the muffins on a microwave-safe dish and top each with the Swiss cheese and walnuts. Microwave for 50 seconds, or until the cheese has melted. In a medium bowl, mix together the yogurt and mixed fruit.

To serve: Plate two muffin halves with 3 tablespoons of the fruit and yogurt mixture and decorate with strawberries and fresh mint sprigs. Serve with maple syrup for topping.

Tips and Variations

*The innkeeper recommends a combination of melons, kiwi, banana, and pineapple.

HENDERSON PARK INN

Henderson Park Inn has been a destination vacation spot for year, but after Hurricane Ivan the inn suffered quite a bit of damage. The inn has been completely renovated and reopened for guests in 2007, something many returning guests were overjoyed to hear.

"… The location next to Henderson Park National Seashore is perfect… we saw a large group of dolphins playing and twirling in the air a little before sunset. The rooms are all comfy and decorated beautifully. When you arrive at the Henderson Park Inn, you will find a tray on your bed with a bottle of wine, opener, glasses, and a plate of grapes. The full Southern breakfast with lots of fresh fruit (and cheese grits!) is yummy, as is the gourmet boxed lunch. Be sure to try the wild salmon sandwich! There is also a happy hour with complimentary beer and wine served between 5 and 6 pm. Top it all off with beachside chairs and umbrellas, complimentary bottled water, sodas, and candy bars… how could anyone not love this place? Oh, and I forgot the best part of all – the customer service is unbelievably wonderful… it is worth every penny!" ~ GUEST

INNKEEPER: Ryan Olin
ADDRESS: 2700 Scenic Hwy 98 E, Destin, Florida 32541
TELEPHONE: (850) 269-8646; (866) 398-4432
E-MAIL: rolin@hendersonparkinn.com
WEBSITE: www.hendersonparkinn.com
ROOMS: 32 Suites; Private baths
CHILDREN: Cannot accommodate
PETS: Not allowed

Garden Eggs Benedict with Basil Hollandaise

Makes 2 Eggs Per Serving

Eggs
Sliced tomato

Potato Pancake:
½ cup chopped onion
¼ cup thinly sliced scallions
1½ cups coarsely grated,
   peeled russet potatoes
½ teaspoon salt
¼ teaspoon freshly ground pepper
2 slices bacon, chopped
¼ cup fresh mozzarella cheese,
   shredded

Basil Hollandais Sauce:
1 cup packed basil leaves
1 stick (½ cup) unsalted butter
2 large egg yolks
4 teaspoons fresh lemon juice
2 teaspoons Dijon-style
   mustard
Salt and freshly ground
   pepper, to taste

Poach eggs as neded.

For the potato pancakes: In a large bowl, combine the onion, scallions, potatoes, salt, pepper, and bacon; fold in the mozzarella. Spread ½ cup of the mixture on an oiled grill or skillet. You can do multiple pancakes at once, make sure they are 2 inches apart. Cook over a moderately low heat, undisturbed, for 20 minutes. Increase the heat and cook for an additional 5-10 minutes, until the undersides are browned. Turn the pancakes and cook for 10 minutes more. Remove from heat and loosely cover with foil; keep warm until ready to serve.

For the basil hollandaise sauce: Melt the butter over moderate heat and keep warm. In a blender or food processor, blend the egg yolks, lemon juice, mustard, and basil leaves for 5 seconds. With the motor running, add the melted butter in a stream and season with salt and pepper.

To serve: Arrange two potato pancakes on a warmed plate and top with sliced tomatoes and poached eggs (one each per pancake). Drizzle with basil hollandaise and garnish with fresh basil sprigs.

Spinach Frittata with Sun-Dried Tomato & Goat Cheese

Makes 4 Servings

9 eggs
2 tablespoons milk
⅓ cup grated Parmesan cheese
2 tablespoons chopped sun-dried tomatoes
Salt and pepper
1 pound baby spinach,
  cleaned with stems removed
1 tablespoon extra-virgin olive oil
1 medium onion, chopped
1 clove garlic, minced
3 ounces goat cheese

Preheat oven to 400°F. In a large bowl, whisk together the eggs, milk, and Parmesan; add the sun-dried tomatoes and season with salt and pepper. Set aside. In a large oven-proof skillet, toss the spinach leaves with a small amount of water. Lightly wilt the leaves until the water has evaporated. Remove the spinach from the pan and set aside. Using the same oven-proof pan, heat olive oil over medium heat and sauté the onions until they are soft and translucent. Add the garlic and stir until it becomes fragrant. Be careful not to brown the garlic. Toss in the wilted spinach.

Spread the spinach mixture evenly over the bottom of the pan. Pour in the egg mixture, gently lifting the edges of the spinach mixture to allow the egg to flow underneath. When the egg is about half-set, sprinkle with the crumbled goat cheese. Place the pan in the preheated oven and bake 10-12 minutes until golden brown and puffy. Allow the frittata to cool for at least 5 minutes before cutting into squares.

A FRITTATA is an Italian omelet that using meats, cheeses and vegetables as filling. They are similar to French omelets, but they are typically first cooked on the stove and hen finished under a broiler. Unlike the French omelet, the frittata is served open-faced. Italians have also been known to bake pasta leftovers into their frittatas.

Other omelet incarnations include the Spanish tortilla de patatas, or an egg omelet with fried potatoes. This variety is a common tapas throughout Spain and can be served warm or cold.

The traditional French omelet is cooked very quickly in a very hot pan. The French omelet is cooked completely in a skillet, without flipping, and is rolled onto the serving plate in a trifold.

Bayfront Marin House B&B Inn

The Bayfront Marin is one of St. Augustine's most interesting historical inns. The building itself consists of pieces from three different historic buildings with the oldest portion of the inn dating back to the 1700s. Other portions of the home were actually Victorian cottages that were purchased and moved to the property in the 1890s by Captain Henry Belknap. Upon the captain's death, the home was sold and converted to individual apartments. The structure passed through various hands until 1988 when the Graubard family purchased the home and made it the inn that it is today.

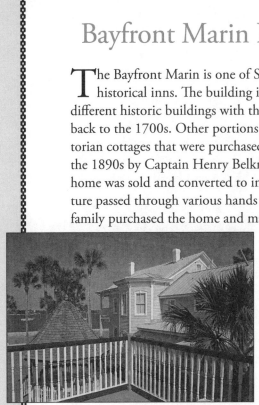

In 2003, the inn was fully renovated and now features fifteen lovely and elegant guest rooms each furnished with period antiques and Victorian décor. Each room is unique but features amenities such as pillow topped beds, private entrances, and terry cloth robes. Guests will also enjoy the full, gourmet breakfast, the early evening wine hour, and the evening dessert selection. Magnificent views of dolphins, sailboats, and the morning sunrise and the picturesque scenery of the Intracoastal waterway, Bridge of Lions, and Castillo de San Marco can all be enjoyed from the porches and courtyards of this luxurious inn.

INNKEEPERS: The Graubard Family

ADDRESS: 142 Avenida Menendez, St. Augustine, Florida 32084

TELEPHONE: (904) 824-4301; (800) 513-9814

E-MAIL: info@bayfrontmarinhouse.com

WEBSITE: www.bayfrontmarinhouse.com

ROOMS: 11 Rooms; 4 Suites; Private baths

CHILDREN: Welcome; Call ahead

PETS: Welcome; Call ahead

Vegetarian Strata

Makes 6 Servings

"More and more frequently, guests are requesting vegetarian breakfast dishes. This is one of the dishes that we serve if we have enough advance notice."
—INNKEEPER, *Bayfront Marin House B&B Inn*

2 slices wheat bread, cubed
¼ cup Swiss cheese
½ cup sliced mushrooms
¼ cup chopped onions
1 clove crushed garlic
½ cup chopped green bell pepper
Salt and pepper
2 tablespoons olive oil
½ cup chopped tomatoes
½ cup snow peas
6 beaten eggs
¾ cup milk
Fresh or dried parsley

Preheat oven to 350°F. Grease a two-quart casserole dish and layer the bread cubes into the bottom; cover with grated cheese. Heat the olive oil in a large skillet over medium-high heat. Sauté the mushrooms, onion, garlic, and green peppers until tender. Stir in the tomatoes and snow peas and sauté an additional 2 minutes. Pour the cooked vegetables over the bread mixture. In a small bowl, mix together the beaten eggs and milk and pour over the cooked vegetables. Bake 45-50 minutes until a knife inserted in the center comes away clean. Let stand a few minutes before sprinkling with parsley and serving.

CAMELLIA ROSE INN

Gainesville, Florida is a sleepy town that's perfect for a great relaxing vacation. Of course, there's still plenty to do in and around the area. Gainesville is home to the Florida Museum of Natural History, The Kanapaha Botanical Gardens, and The Samuel P. Harn Museum of Art. And, Gainesville is a college town so there's plenty of hot night spots to hit up before returning to the Camel-

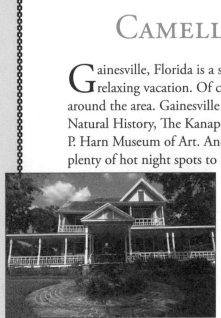

lia Rose Inn. Pat and Tom will gladly recommend some of their own favorite restaurants and activities as well. Whether it's just you and that special someone or a weekend retreat for the whole family, Pat and Tom will help you plan the best vacation to suit your every need.

"I called the Camellia Rose [Inn] on very short notice. Fortunately, Pat & Tom were able to accommodate us. The inn is absolutely beautiful! I was overjoyed at the cleanliness, every surface was spotless. Breakfast was lovingly prepared by Pat and was better than any restaurant breakfast I have ever had. She asked about any dietary restrictions (I am a vegetarian) and provided plenty of delicious and substantial options. The entire experience was flawless and I would wholeheartedly recommend [this inn] to anyone. My husband was hoping Pat & Tom might adopt him! We will never stay anywhere else in Gainesville…" —GUEST

INNKEEPERS:	Pat & Tom McCants
ADDRESS:	205 SE 7th Street, Gainesville, Florida 32601
TELEPHONE:	(352) 395-7673
E-MAIL:	info@camelliaroseinn.com
WEBSITE:	www.camelliaroseinn.com
ROOMS:	6 Rooms; 1 Cottage; Private baths
CHILDREN:	Welcome
PETS:	Welcome; Call ahead; Resident pets

Vegetable Breakfast Strata

Plan ahead, this dish needs to refrigerate overnight!
Makes 6-8 Servings

1 tablespoon oil
1 large sweet onion, halved and thinly sliced
1 large red bell pepper, diced
1 large Yukon Gold potato, peeled and diced
1 (12 ounce) sourdough loaf, cubed
1 (8 ounce) round of Brie, rind removed and
    cut into ½-inch cubes, or 2 cups shredded Swiss
1 cup shredded Parmesan cheese
8 large eggs
3 cups milk
2 tablespoons Dijon mustard
1 teaspoon seasoned salt
1 teaspoon pepper

Heat the oil in a large skillet over medium-high heat; add the onion, bell pepper, and potato and sauté 10-12 minutes, until vegetables are tender and onion slices begin to turn golden-brown.

Grease a 13x9-inch baking dish and layer in half of the bread cubes, half of the vegetables, half of the Brie or Swiss, and half of the Parmesan. In a medium bowl, whisk together the eggs, milk, mustard, seasoned salt, and pepper. Pour half of the egg mixture over the strata. Repeat layers and pour the remaining egg mixture over the top. Cover and chill 8-24 hours.

The following morning: Preheat oven to 350°F and bake, uncovered, for 45-50 minutes, or until lightly browned on top and set in center.

Tips and Variations

You can substitute roasted red peppers in place of fresh if you prefer.

Grady House
Bed & Breakfast

In 2008, Grady House was voted one of the Top 3 Best Breakfast in Gainesville, and the Best Bed & Breakfast in Florida. This is all thanks to the welcoming atmosphere and the warmth and hospitality of host and hostess, Paul and Luce Regensdorf. Guests will love the extra-special touches that come with a stay at this historic inn. Each morning, you'll wake to the mouthwatering smells of Lucie's

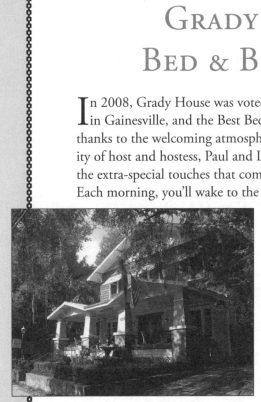

home cooked breakfasts. Then, you can spend your afternoon lounging in the garden with a good book and a glass of wine before retiring to a cozy featherbed and luxurious linens. Some guests have reported possible hauntings at the Grady House. Don't worry though, others say that a kind and gentle ghost may tuck you in at night.

"We spent a relaxing and luxurious Mothers' Day weekend at the Grady House ... The gardens are spectacular ... Breakfasts were delicious and because it was Mothers' Day, included mimosas and a rose for each mother. Our hosts clearly enjoy extending hospitality. We will definitely go again!" ~ GUEST

INNKEEPERS:	Paul & Lucie Regensdorf
ADDRESS:	420 NW 1st Avenue, High Springs, Florida 32643
TELEPHONE:	(386) 454-2206
E-MAIL:	gradyhouse@gradyhouse.com
WEBSITE:	www.gradyhouse.com
ROOMS:	2 Rooms; 3 Suites; 1 Cottage
CHILDREN:	Children age 10 and older welcome
PETS:	Not allowed; Resident pets

High Springs Farmer's Market Veggie Strata

Makes 6-8 Servings

"The High Springs Farmer's Market asked me to make a dish using locally grown vegetables and to provide samples and a copy of the recipe. I created this dish along with a roasted vegetable lasagna and served them both to visitors at the Farmer's Market."

—INNKEEPER, *Grady House Historic Bed & Breakfast*

4 garlic cloves, minced
1 cup diced bread
4 tablespoons extra virgin olive oil
1 cup chopped red onion
½ cup chopped red bell pepper
½ cup chopped yellow bell pepper
½ cup chopped green pepper
1 small crookneck squash, chopped
½ pound spinach leaves

½ pound baby bella mushrooms
8 large eggs
2 cups half & half, or whole milk
2 cups grated mozzarella cheese
¼ cup grated Parmesan cheese
¼ cup grated Romano cheese
Salt and pepper
1 teaspoon dried oregano
½ pint grape tomatoes, halved

Preheat oven to 350°F. In a baking dish, toss together 2 of the minced garlic cloves, the bread cubes, and 2 tablespoons of the olive oil. Bake, stirring once, 8-10 minutes, or until lightly toasted; set aside. Heat 1 tablespoon of olive oil in a large skillet over medium heat; add the onion, peppers, and squash and sauté 6-7 minutes. Season with salt and pepper and remove to a plate until read for use. Using the same skillet, sauté the remaining 2 garlic cloves in 1 tablespoon of olive oil. Add the mushrooms and sauté 6-7 minutes until softened; season with salt and pepper.

Place the baked bread cubes into a lightly oiled 9x13-inch baking dish. Pour the sautéed peppers and onion over the top. Layer the spinach leaves over the top of the vegetables and top with the mushrooms. Spread the cheeses over the top of the entire casserole. In a large bowl, whisk together the eggs and milk and pour over the cheese layer. Place the halved grape tomatoes on top of the casserole and bake until set, 40-50 minutes. Let stand 10 minutes before cutting in squares to serve.

LONGBOARD INN AND NUNS & ROSES

Each guest room at the Longboard Inn and Nuns & Roses has its own personality and charm. Local art – stained glass, ceramics, water colors… – fill each room. Private whirlpool baths, queen sized hand-crafted beds, and unique hand-painted furniture are just a few of the many draws at these inns. Your charming host and hostess and their genial staff want your vacation experience here to be a memorable one that will have you returning for many years in the future.

" I can't say enough about how wonderful this property is. The rooms are eclectic and charming, as are the proprietors. The breakfast was gourmet – a delicious casserole with eggs, hash browns, apples, a fruit salad, and a basket of fresh-baked rolls and muffins. [John and Dee] are very knowledgeable about the area and quite friendly. They made us feel at home from the moment that we arrived… I want to go back again and again… You won't regret booking your stay at the Longboard Inn!" —GUEST

INNKEEPERS: John & Dee Green

ADDRESS: 312 Washington Street, New Smyrna Beach, Florida 32168

TELEPHONE: (386) 428-3499; (888) 655-2025

E-MAIL: info@longboardinn.com

WEBSITE: www.longboardinn.com

ROOMS: 6 Suites; 2 Cottages; Private baths

CHILDREN: Children age 12 and older welcome

PETS: Welcome; Resident pets

Longboard Inn Veggie Delight

Makes 12 Servings

1 tablespoon olive oil
1 medium onion, chopped
1 medium green bell pepper, chopped
3 tablespoons butter
1 clove garlic, minced
8 mushrooms, chopped
Salt and pepper, to taste
4 eggs
1½ cups milk
½ cup flour
2 tablespoons fresh basil
2 tablespoons chopped fresh rosemary
2 ounces grated Cheddar cheese
1 ounce roughly crumbled Feta cheese
1 ounce grated Romano

Preheat oven to 400°F. Heat the oil in a large non-stick skillet over medium-high heat. Add the onion and green pepper and sauté until soft. Add 1 tablespoon of butter, the garlic, and the mushrooms to the pan and cook an additional 3 minutes, stirring often. Season the vegetables with salt and pepper, to taste. Remove from heat and set aside. Grease 12 small baking dishes with the remaining butter and spoon an even amount of the onion/mushroom mixture into each one.

In a medium bowl, whisk together the eggs and milk until the mixture is frothy; mix in the flour. Stir in the herbs, Cheddar, and Feta and pour over the onion mixture and sprinkle with Romano cheese Bake 15 minutes, or until puffed up and golden. Let stand 10 minutes. Garnish with parsley and serve.

St. Francis Inn

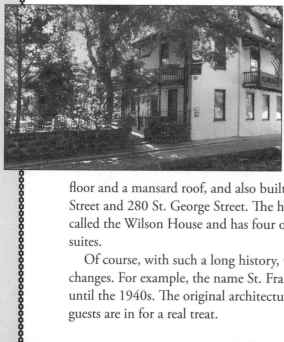

Just around the corner from St. Augustine's picturesque oldest house you'll find what is unquestionably St. Augustine's "oldest inn." The St. Francis dates back to 1791 when Gaspar Garcia, a sergeant in the Third Battalion of the Infantry Regiment of Cuba was granted the lot by the King of Spain. Architecture at the time reflected the King's constant concern in regards to the threat of possible invasion. Houses had to be built in such a way that the residents and the town could be defended as if by a fortress.

The inn was first converted from a single residence to lodging in 1845. In 1888, philanthropist John L. Wilson purchased the inn and began renovations. He added a third floor and a mansard roof, and also built the homes at 34 St. Francis Street and 280 St. George Street. The house on St. George is still called the Wilson House and has four of the St. Francis Inn's guest suites.

Of course, with such a long history, the inn has undergone many changes. For example, the name St. Francis Inn was not adopted until the 1940s. The original architecture still remains, though, and guests are in for a real treat.

INNKEEPERS:	Joe & Margaret Finnegan
ADDRESS:	279 St. George Street, St. Augustine, Florida 32084
TELEPHONE:	(904) 824-6068; (800) 824-6062
E-MAIL:	innkeeper@stfrancisinn.com
WEBSITE:	www.stfrancisinn.com
ROOMS:	12 Rooms; 4 Suites; 1 Cottage; Private baths
CHILDREN:	Call ahead
PETS:	Small pets welcome; Call ahead; Resident pets

Five Cheese Strata

Plan ahead, this dish needs to refrigerate at least 1 hour, or overnight!
Makes 12 Servings

"A guest favorite!"
—INNKEEPER, *St. Francis Inn*

½ cup shredded Colby Cheddar cheese
½ cup shredded Parmesan cheese
½ cup shredded Mozzarella cheese
½ cup shredded Swiss cheese
½ cup shredded Jack Cheddar cheese
10 large eggs, beaten
2 cups milk

Spray a 13x9-inch baking dish with non-stick cooking spray. Combine the cheeses and pour into the bottom of the prepared dish. In a large bowl, whisk together the eggs and milk. Pour the egg mixture over the cheese and cover the dish. Refrigerate at least one hour, or overnight.

To bake: Remove the dish from the fridge and preheat oven to 350°F. Remove covering and replace with foil, the underside (side facing the eggs) should be sprayed with non-stick cooking spray. Bake 45 minutes, remove foil and bake an additional 10 minutes, or until the strata is set.

Frescatta Italian Strata

Plan ahead, this dish needs to refrigerate at least 1 hour, or overnight!
Makes 12 Servings

6 ounces baby spinach
½ cup Parmesan cheese
2 Roma tomatoes, sliced
1 cup mozzarella cheese
10 large eggs, beaten
2 cups milk
1 tablespoon basil pesto

Spray a 13x9-inch casserole dish with non-stick cooking spray. Place the spinach evenly along the bottom of the pan. Top with the Parmesan cheese, then the sliced tomatoes, and finally the mozzarella. In a large bowl, combine the beaten eggs, milk, and basil pesto and pour over the mozzarella. Cover and refrigerate at least one hour, or overnight.

To bake: Remove the dish from the fridge and preheat oven to 350°F. Bake uncovered for 50-60 minutes, or until the center is set.

Chef's Eggs

Makes 9 Servings

12 large eggs
3 tablespoons melted butter
½ cup flour
2 teaspoons baking powder
12 ounces cottage cheese
3 cups shredded Monterey Jack cheese
1 (4 ounce) can chopped green chiles, drained
2 Roma tomatoes, sliced

Preheat oven to 350°F. In a large bowl, whisk together the eggs, melted butter, flour, and baking soda. Stir in the cottage cheese, Monterey Jack, and green chiles. Pour the mixture into a greased 9x13-inch pan and bake 10 minutes. Remove from the oven and place the tomato slices evenly around the pan. Return the dish to the oven and bake 20 minutes longer. Cut into slices and serve.

THE OLD POWDER HOUSE INN

Once you visit the Old Powder House Inn, you'll never want to leave. Guests have been returning here year after year to enjoy historic St. Augustine and the fabulous hospitality of the inn. From the mouthwatering breakfast to the elegant décor, this inn is truly a wonderful place to stay. Each of the inn's nine elegant guest rooms features its own unique theme and complementing décor. Hardwood flooring, period antiques, luxury linens, and two wonderful hosts, will make your stay here a memorable and exciting one. And don't forget, you're still in the heart of historic St. Augustine. Everything – shopping, dining, beaches, and historic tourist attractions – are all within quick reach.

"[My recent stay at The Old Powder House] was my eleventh stay at this property. That in itself speaks volumes about my affection for St. Augustine in general and this excellent little b&b in particular. The rooms are comfortable and well appointed. The breakfast has to be among the best a traveler will ever find. The porches, particularly the upstairs porch, are quite simply the place where stress goes to die. This might be the most welcoming house you'll ever walk into…" —GUEST

INNKEEPERS: Katie & Kal Kalieta
ADDRESS: 38 Cordova Street, St. Augustine, Florida 32084
TELEPHONE: (904) 824-4149; (800) 447-4149
E-MAIL: innkeeper@oldpowderhouse.com
WEBSITE: www.oldpowderhouse.com
ROOMS: 9 Rooms; 2 Suites; Private baths
CHILDREN: Children age 8 and older welcome
PETS: Not allowed

Three Cheese Florentine

Makes 24 Servings

*"Defrost your spinach overnight. The following morning,
before you begin assembling the casserole, thoroughly drain the
spinach and pat down with paper towels to remove excess moisture.
You could also cook the spinach in the microwave
until just defrosted and drain thoroughly before use."*

—INNKEEPER, *The Old Powder House Inn*

2 (10 ounce) packages frozen chopped spinach
24 eggs
1 (24 ounce) package small curd cottage cheese
16 ounces feta cheese with tomato and basil
2 cups shredded Cheddar cheese
2 cups grated Parmesan cheese
2 cups chopped ham, bacon, or sausage (optional)
6 tablespoons melted butter
2 tablespoons all-purpose flour
1 tablespoon Worcestershire sauce
1 teaspoon dill
½ teaspoon white pepper
½ teaspoon garlic salt

Preheat oven to 350°F and spray two 9x13-inch glass baking
dishes with non-stick cooking spray. In a large bowl, beat the
eggs, then, fold in the following ingredients one at a time: the
cottage cheese, feta cheese, and 1 cup each of the Cheddar and
Parmesan cheeses, spinach, and meat if using. In a separate bowl,
mix together the melted butter, flour, Worcestershire sauce, dill,
white pepper, and garlic salt; fold into the egg mixture.

Divide the mixture evenly between the two pans and sprinkle
generously with the remaining Cheddar and Parmesan cheese.
Bake 50 minutes, or until the center is set and a toothpick comes
away clean.

Tips and Variations

This recipe can easily be halved for smaller preparation.

Turtle Beach Inn & Cottages at Indian Pass

Each room at the Turtle Beach Inn has been individually decorated with comfort and relaxation in mind. Every morning guests will enjoy a serve-yourself breakfast (no set time which means that you can sleep in!) of fresh fruit, homemade breads and muffins and hot items like Trish's Florentine Eggs. Canoeing, kayaking, fishing,

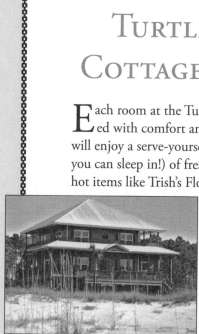

swimming, horseback riding, boat tours, and golf are just a few of the activities that are available nearby and Apalachicola with its great dining and shopping is just a short drive away.

"My husband and I went to Turtle Beach Inn for a lovely weekend away. What we found [there] was a great combination of beach house and B&B. The inn is very small, only four rooms, all with outside entrances from the wraparound porch (which keeps things quiet and private). Everything is comfortably decorated and [the hosts] are gracious and knowledgeable. Breakfast was a tasty selection of cereals, toast, fruit, juice, and a homemade hot dish… The inn has all you want in a beach house: beach towels, chairs, boogie boards, hot tub, plenty of nooks for reading of just relaxing, hammock… you name it. And, it's right on the beach so you fall asleep to the sound of the waves. Heaven!" —Guest

INNKEEPER: Trish Petrie

ADDRESS: 140 Painted Pony Road, Port St. Joe, Florida 32456

TELEPHONE: (850) 229-9366

E-MAIL: info@turtlebeachinn.com

WEBSITE: www.turtlebeachinn.com

ROOMS: 4 Rooms; 3 Cottages; Private & shared baths

CHILDREN: Welcome; Call ahead

PETS: Not allowed; Resident pets

Eggs Florentine

Makes 8 Servings

"This is an absolutely delicious dish;
the recipe was given to me by a guest
who stayed at the inn. This is a great vegetarian option,
truly a Turtle Beach Inn "green egg" dish!"
—INNKEEPER, *Turtle Beach Inn*

9 whole eggs
2 cups cottage cheese
2 cups grated Swiss cheese
8 ounces Feta cheese
4 tablespoons melted butter
2 (10 ounce) packages chopped spinach,
    drained
1 teaspoon nutmeg

Preheat oven to 365°F and grease a 9x13-inch baking dish.
Mix the eggs, cottage cheese, Swiss cheese, feta cheese, and butter
together in a large bowl. Add the chopped spinach and nutmeg
and stir to combine. Pour the whole mixture into the prepared
dish and bake 1 hour, until set.

Tips and Variations

You could also use fresh spinach if you like.
Soak the leaves in a sink-ful of water, remove and pat dry.

Sausage Brunch Casserole

Makes 12 Servings

"This is another Turtle Beach staple.
The recipe was adapted from one found in Southern Living."
—*INNKEEPER, Turtle Beach Inn*

1½ pounds ground pork sausage
1 (8 ounce) package refrigerated crescent roll dough
2 cups mozzarella cheese
4 eggs, beaten
¾ cup milk
Salt and pepper, to taste

Preheat oven to 425°F. Cook the sausage in a large deep skillet over medium-high heat. Once the sausage is evenly browned, drain and crumble; set aside. Lightly grease a 9x13-inch baking dish. Lay the crescent rolls flat over the bottom of the dish. In a large bowl, combine the sausage, cheese, eggs, milk, and salt and pepper. Pour the mixture over the crescent rolls and bake 15 minutes. The casserole should be bubbly and the crescent rolls baked through.

CASSEROLES come in many different types. They are typically very easy and time-effective. Most can be prepared the beforehand and baked when needed. Items are layered into a baking dish and cooked in the oven. Breakfast, lunch, and dinner casseroles are quite common these days, and some say that this is thanks to the rise in condensed and canned soups in the 1950s. Casseroles come in a wide variety and virtually every region of the world has their own versions. Quite simply, a casserole means a dish that is "served in the vessel used for cooking" per the culinary term, *en casserole.*

Mount Dora Historic Inn

Innkeepers, Jim and Ana Tuttle, know that vacationers are looking for more than just a place to rest their heads at night. Their every attention to detail will make you feel like you've been welcomed into the family. Breakfast is just part of this experience, and is absolutely not to be missed. Each morning, Jim will delight your palate with one of his own signature creations. Items are always changing but include selections like stuffed French toast, breakfast soufflés, omelets, and sweet potato pancakes.

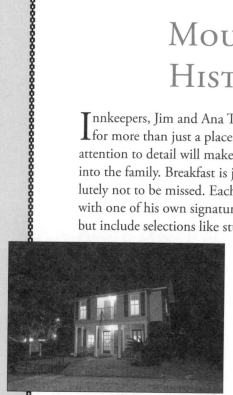

"We recently found a gem in Mount Dora, Florida. My husband and I were looking for a quiet getaway that was not too far from our kids in Miami and we found the PERFECT PLACE… The innkeepers, Jim and Ana, were fabulous. Jim's gourmet breakfast was phenomenal and Anna's detailed housekeeping touches made us feel like royalty. There is so much to do right outside your door and when you're done and return to the inn, Jim has baked one of his special treats for a late night snack…. Jim and Ana's hospitality go above and beyond what you would expect. We had a weekend we will never forget." — GUEST

INNKEEPERS:	Jim & Ana Tuttle
ADDRESS:	221 East 4th Avenue, Mount Dora, Florida 32757
TELEPHONE:	(352) 735-1212; (800) 927-6344
E-MAIL:	innkeepermdhi@comcast.net
WEBSITE:	www.mountdorahistoricinn.com
ROOMS:	4 Rooms; Private baths
CHILDREN:	Welcome; Call ahead
PETS:	Welcome; Call ahead

Jim's Sausage Soufflé

Makes 5 Servings

10 hen's eggs, separated
4 ounces sour cream
$\frac{1}{3}$ cup whole milk
1 teaspoon dry mustard
4 dashes hot sauce, Tabasco recommended
Black pepper, to taste
¼ teaspoon fresh ground nutmeg
4 ounces shredded Cheddar cheese
4 ounces shredded Muenster cheese
2 ounces shredded Swiss cheese
½ pound bulk sausage, cooked, chopped and drained

Preheat oven to 350°F. In a medium bowl, whip the egg whites until stiff peaks begin to form. In a separate large bowl, whip together the egg yolks, sour cream, and milk. Add the mustard, hot sauce, pepper, and nutmeg and mix well. Carefully fold in the egg whites. Add the cheeses and the sausage and mix until wet and well distributed. Pour the mixture into a well greased soufflé dish or a ramekin just large enough to contain the mixture. Bake 60-70 minutes. Or, you can check the internal temperature of the soufflé using an instant read thermometer. The temperature should be 180°F. This will cause your soufflé to fall faster than normal, though.

ALLING HOUSE

This circa 1908 home was originally purchased in 1918 by Mr. and Mrs. Edward B. Alling. Alling, a four-time mayor of Orange City in the 1920s, donated land for the town's city hall and even helped lead the construction of the building. The couple lived in the French Avenue home for over 50 years.

When current owners Gerald and Nan purchased the home with dreams of converting it to a b&b, they knew that preserving the history of the building had to be at the top of their list. After

over a year of laborious and loving restorations, Alling House opened its doors to guests in September 2004.

Each guest room at the inn features a unique design scheme courtesy of Nan herself. Guests love the heart pine floors and Victorian décor that can be found throughout. Relaxing in the peaceful setting may be exactly what you're looking for, but there are also plenty of activities just minutes from the inn. Kayaking, canoeing, and manatee watching are just a few things to do at nearby St. Johns River and Blue Springs State Park and Deland's main street has plenty of antiquing and dining options.

INNKEEPERS:	Gerald & Nan Hill
ADDRESS:	215 E. French Avenue, Orange City, Florida 32763
TELEPHONE:	(386) 775-7648
E-MAIL:	info@allinghousebb.com
WEBSITE:	www.allinghousebb.com
ROOMS:	3 Rooms; 5 Cottages; Private baths
CHILDREN:	Welcome
PETS:	Welcome; Resident pet

Hash Brown Bake

Makes 4 Servings

"This casserole recipe was adapted to be used for individual guests on an as needed basis and can be customized according to tastes and dietary needs."
—INNKEEPER, *Alling House B&B*

Cooking spray
8 cups, ready-to-cook hash brown potatoes
   with peppers and onions, thawed
2 cups shredded mild Cheddar cheese
8 eggs
½ cup milk
½ teaspoon salt
½ teaspoon pepper

Preheat oven to 350°F. Spray four individual sized ramekins with non-stick cooking spray. Put ½ cup hash brown potatoes into the bottom of each dish and top with ½ cup cheese. Place a second layer of hash brown potatoes (½ cup) over the cheese.

In a small bowl, mix 4 eggs with milk salt and pepper and divide equally between the dishes. Bake for 25 minutes.

Remove from oven and top each dish with one poached egg.

Tips and Variations

To poach eggs: In a large sauce pan, heat 3-4 cups of water until almost boiling. Add 1 tablespoon of vinegar to the water (vinegar helps the egg to maintain its shape). Crack each egg into a small dish and slide the individual egg into the water. You should be able to cook about 4 eggs at a time. Keep water just below a boil, reducing heat as needed, and cook until egg whites are set but centers are still soft.

BEACH DRIVE INN

On the North end of St. Petersburg's Beach Drive, at the edge of the Historic Old Northeast, sits the lovely and elegant Beach Drive Inn. The home is believed to have been built in 1910, but all records previous to 1913 were lost when the county court house burned. Regardless, this historic inn has been meticulously maintained and innkeepers Roland and Heather pride themselves on their special attention to every detail. Each room features all new décor geared towards providing you the perfect soothing atmosphere.

Beach Drive Inn is conveniently located walking distance from much of St. Petersburg's area attractions including shopping, dining, and local events. Enjoy the inn's wine and cheese welcome nights and a full-course hearty breakfast before setting off to explore St. Petersburg.

"This charming b&b was in the heart of everything ...
The owners were absolutely wonderful and helpful.
I have traveled the world, but this was the best vacation we have had.
I will be back to visit again!" —GUEST

INNKEEPERS: Roland & Heather Martino

ADDRESS: 532 Beach Drive NE, St. Petersburg, Florida 33701

TELEPHONE: (727) 822-2244

E-MAIL: info@beachdriveinn.com

WEBSITE: www.beachdriveinn.com

ROOMS: 4 Rooms; 2 Suites; Private baths

CHILDREN: Children age 12 and older welcome

PETS: Small pets welcome; Resident pets

Brunch Delight

Makes 6-8 Servings

1 tablespoon olive oil
4 cups potatoes, cut into ½ inch cubes
¾ cup shredded Monterey Jack cheese
1 cup diced cooked ham or Canadian bacon
¼ cup sliced green onions
4 eggs, beaten, or 1 cup egg substitute
½ cup milk
¼ teaspoon pepper

Preheat oven to 350°F. Grease a 2-quart baking dish with the olive oil. Arrange the cubed potatoes evenly in the dish; bake in preheated oven for 10 minutes. Remove dish from the oven and stir the potatoes. Sprinkle the cheese, ham, and green onions over the cooked potatoes.

In a small bowl, mix together the beaten eggs, milk, and pepper. Pour the egg mixture over the potatoes. At this point, the casserole may be covered and stored in the refrigerator overnight.

Bake uncovered for 40-45 minutes, or until the potatoes are tender. Serve with fresh fruit.

Tips and Variations

Honey maple ham also makes a good addition.

Carriage Way B&B

Built between 1883 and 1885, the Carriage Way B&B is one of the most elegant and romantic inns in all of Florida. The traditional Victorian home was fully renovated in 1984 after having been converted to individual apartments in the 1940s. Each of the inn's 11 rooms are named for the home's previous owners, occupants, and others who have played an important part in the history of the

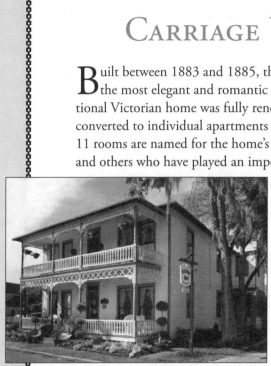

building. Antiques, family heirlooms, and carefully chosen reproductions can be found throughout the inn adding to the historic and romantic atmosphere throughout.

Conveniently located within the heart of St. Augustine, guests will find plenty of activities around the inn to keep them occupied – if they decide to leave even for the day, that is. Just steps from the inn is the famed St. George Street, the walking mall, quaint shops, museums, and historic sites. You can even book a carriage ride that will pick you up right at Carriage Way's front door. There are also plenty of dining options in the area, or you can arrange to have the inn fix you up a gourmet picnic basket to take down to the beach.

INNKEEPERS: Bill Johnson & sons, Larry & John
ADDRESS: 70 Cuna Street, St. Augustine, Florida 32084
TELEPHONE: (904) 829-2467; (800) 908-9832
E-MAIL: info@carriageway.com
WEBSITE: www.carriageway.com
ROOMS: 11 Rooms; 1 Cottage; Private baths
CHILDREN: Children age 8 and older welcome
PETS: Not allowed

Parmesan Artichoke Casserole

Makes 12 Servings

*"This is a guest favorite and
is one of our most highly requested breakfast entrées."*
—INNKEEPER, *Carriage Way B&B*

8 eggs
½ cup flour
1 teaspoon garlic pepper
12 ounces shredded Monterey Jack cheese
1½ cups cottage cheese
2 (4 ounce) cans green chilies
½ can artichoke hearts, quartered
1 cup freshly grated Parmesan cheese

Preheat oven to 350°F and grease a 13x9-inch baking dish. Beat the eggs for 4 minutes; mix in the flour, garlic pepper, Monterey Jack and cottage cheeses, and green chilies. Pour the mixture into the greased dish. Arrange the quartered artichoke hearts over the top and sprinkle the entire dish with Parmesan cheese. Bake 40 minutes.

Did you know that the artichoke is actually a flower bud? It's true. If allowed to flower, the violet-blue blossoms will measure up to seven inches in diameter.

PARK CIRCLE B&B

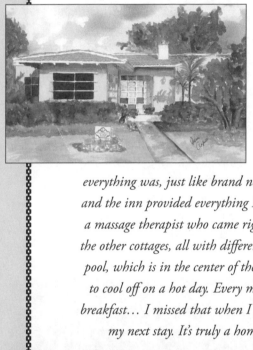

Park Circle is one of the most unique lodging experiences Florida has to offer. Located in North Redington Beach, the inn is actually a group of beach houses that ring a central pool. Whether you're looking for a great family destination or a romantic place for you and your sweetheart, Park Circle is able to accommodate both. Each guest house has its own personality and decorating scheme. They also range in size. The smallest can comfortably house up to four and the largest can accommodate up to eight.

"I highly recommend [Park Circle]. I was very impressed by how clean everything was, just like brand new! The cottage was very comfortable and the inn provided everything I needed for a relaxing stay including a massage therapist who came right to the property. I viewed many of the other cottages, all with different décor and each one was lovely. The pool, which is in the center of the property, was just that added touch to cool off on a hot day. Every morning I anticipated the wonderful breakfast… I missed that when I got home! I am so looking forward to my next stay. It's truly a home away from home." —GUEST

INNKEEPERS: Margaret Bourgeois & Peter Arps

ADDRESS: 16609 Gulf Boulevard, North Redington Beach, Florida 33708

TELEPHONE: (727) 394-8608; (866) 440-7275

E-MAIL: info@parkcircle.com

WEBSITE: www.parkcircle.com

ROOMS: 7 Vacation homes; Private baths

CHILDREN: Welcome

PETS: Not allowed

Eggs Parmesan

Makes 8 Servings

"This is a wonderful presentation!
A great dish for those on low-carb diets."
—INNKEEPER, *Park Circle B&B*

1 pound fresh asparagus
8 thin slices prosciutto
16 large eggs
Salt
Fresh ground pepper
8 ounces shredded Italian cheese blend
¼ cup grated Parmesan cheese
¼ pound butter, slivered

Preheat oven to 450°F and spray 8 gratin dishes with non-stick cooking spray. Cut the tough, woody stems off of the asparagus and discard. Place the asparagus in a pot of salted boiling water and cook 3-4 minutes. Drain and immediately place them in a bath of ice water to set the color. Drain and pat dry. Arrange 3-4 spears of asparagus in each dish and top with 1 slice of prosciutto. Break two eggs into each dish and season lightly with salt and pepper. Divide the cheese blend and Parmesan evenly among the dishes. Top with the slivered butter and bake 8-10 minutes before serving.

THE MERMAID & THE ALLIGATOR

The beautiful Mermaid & Alligator in Old Town Key West is a charming and warm 1904 Victorian mansion with nine guest rooms and suites, and an additional cottage for rental. Each room has a unique design scheme and romantic personality. This enchanting b&b has been gaining increased recognition since it first opened in the late nineties. It's even made the list of *Travel & Leisure's* 30 Great Inns. The tropical setting and traditional b&b hospitality make for a wonderful combination.

A hearty and full breakfast is served each morning to get you ready for whatever your day may hold. If the beach is your destination, try some snorkeling or diving, tour Key West's shops and galleries or just stay in and relax in the poolside chairs beneath the lush and exotic garden.

INNKEEPERS: Dean Carlson & Paul Hayes

ADDRESS: 729 Truman Avenue, Key West, Florida 33040

TELEPHONE: (305) 294-1894; (800) 773-1894

E-MAIL: kwmermaid@aol.com

WEBSITE: www.kwmermaid.com

ROOMS: 9 Rooms; 3 Suites; 1 Cottage; Private baths

CHILDREN: Children age 16 and older welcome

PETS: Not allowed; Resident pets

Eggs Monterey

Makes 16-18 Servings

"This recipe was adapted from a National Egg Counsel recipe."
—INNKEEPER, *The Mermaid & The Alligator*

3½ cups frozen hash brown potato shreds
1 (10 ounce) can Ro-Tel tomatoes, original or hot
3 cups shredded Mexican cheese
1 cup diced green bell pepper
½ cup sliced green onion
½ cup corn
6 cups liquid egg product*
Salt and pepper

Preheat oven to 325°F. In a large mixing bowl, combine the hash browns, tomatoes, cheese, bell pepper, green onion, and corn. Pour in the egg product and mix to combine. Spray two 9-inch pie plates with non-stick cooking spray and divide the mixture evenly between the two. Bake 35-40 minutes, or until puffy and golden.

Tips and Variations

If using a non-convection oven, bake at 350°F for 40-50 minutes.

*14 eggs plus ¾ cup milk whisked together

BAYFRONT WESTCOTT
HOUSE B&B INN

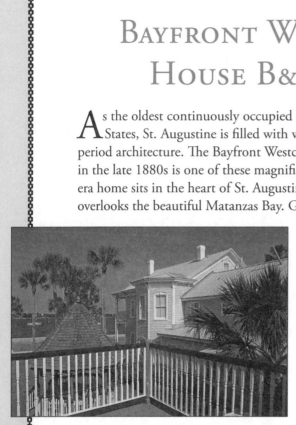

As the oldest continuously occupied European city in the United States, St. Augustine is filled with wonderful examples of period architecture. The Bayfront Westcott, a Victorian home built in the late 1880s is one of these magnificent buildings. This Flagler era home sits in the heart of St. Augustine's historic district and overlooks the beautiful Matanzas Bay. Guests can enjoy the inn's gourmet breakfast while watching the sailboats pass through the bay, or you may also elect to enjoy your breakfast en suite.

The convenient location of the Westcott House is great for guests who want to see the sites of St. Augustine. Museums, restaurants, shops, all the best historic sites, the beach, and the marina are all just a short walk away. The Graubard family recommends biking or walking, and will provide bicycles to all of their guests. See the sites in town, or enjoy a plethora of water activities such as parasailing, skiing, canoeing, deep sea and charter fishing.

INNKEEPERS: The Graubard Family
ADDRESS: 146 Avenida Menendez, St. Augustine, Florida 32084
TELEPHONE: (904) 824-4301; (800) 513-9814
E-MAIL: info@westcotthouse.com
WEBSITE: www.westcotthouse.com
ROOMS: 11 Rooms; 4 Suites; Private baths
CHILDREN: Welcome; Call ahead
PETS: Welcome; Call ahead

Hungarian Eggs Casserole

Makes 18 Servings

"Our chef, Andrea, her husband, Zeko,
and three of their daughters work with us at the inn.
They are from Hungary and are a lovely addition to our staff.
This is Andrea's recipe."

—INNKEEPER, *Bayfront Westcott House B&B Inn*

2 onions
Dash paprika
3 tablespoons oil
1 pound chopped turkey
Salt and pepper
2 chopped green bell peppers
2 chopped tomatoes
1 pint sour cream
14 eggs
2 (1-pound) bags frozen hash brown potatoes
1 pound grated Cheddar cheese
Fresh or dried parsley

Preheat oven to 350°F. In a large skillet over medium-high heat, fry the onions in the oil with the paprika. Add the turkey, salt, and pepper. Cook for about 15 minutes before adding the bell pepper and tomatoes; cook an additional 5 minutes. Turn of the heat and add the sour cream.

Layer the hash brown potatoes into the bottom of a large baking dish. Top with half of the beaten eggs. Spread half of the turkey mixture over the egg layer and sprinkle with a layer of cheese. Repeat with a second layer of the eggs, the turkey mixture, and the cheese. Sprinkle with a bit of fresh or dried parsley and bake 45 minutes.

Our House of
St. Augustine

After a hearty, home-cooked breakfast and some quiet time enjoying the peaceful atmosphere, you might be ready to venture into historic St. Augustine. Innkeeper Dave Brezing can tell you about all the places you absolutely must see while you're there. The inn is located near the San Marcos antique district – the inn's own fabulous selection of antiques came from these shops. Just a short walk will take you to the Castillo de San Marcos fortress and the Matanzas waterfront. Visit the Ancient City's historic sites, shops, and restaurants, or visit the white-sand Atlantic Ocean beaches. At the end of the day, escape back to the warmth and comfort of your room at Our House.

"A weekend away doesn't get better than this! Any preconceived ideas of dowdy b&bs are thrown out the window with the chic, lovely, peaceful setting of Our House. The grounds are impeccably maintained and our private porch was just what we needed at the end of a day of sun, shopping, and exploring.... This place is not to be missed during your visit to St. Augustine." —GUEST

INNKEEPER:	Dave Brezing
ADDRESS:	7 Cincinnati Avenue, St. Augustine, Florida 32084
TELEPHONE:	(904) 347-6260
E-MAIL:	ourhouse@ourhouseofstaugustine.com
WEBSITE:	www.ourhouseofstaugustine.com
ROOMS:	5 Rooms; Private baths
CHILDREN:	Children age 14 and older welcome
PETS:	Not allowed

Baked Eggs Français

Makes 6 Servings

2 tablespoons melted butter
Approximately ½ cup heavy cream
18 mini-toasts
    (such as Ile de France petit pain grille)
    or 6¼-inch thick slices of French baguette
9 large eggs
2 teaspoons Herbes to Provence
Dash freshly ground sea salt
Dash freshly ground black pepper
Dash ground nutmeg

Preheat oven to 350°F. Spray 6 5-inch crème brûlée ramekins with non-stick cooking spray. Pour an even amount of the melted butter into each of the ramekins. Pour about 1½ tablespoons of the heavy cream into each ramekin, just enough to cover the bottoms. Arrange three mini-toasts in each ramekin. If you are using the baguettes instead, use one slice per ramekin.

In a medium bowl, using a fork or a whisk, beat together the eggs, Herbes to Provence, salt, pepper, and nutmeg. Divide the egg mixture evenly between the ramekins. Bake 15-20 minutes, until the eggs are cooked and have puffed up. You'll need to watch these for the last few minutes to make sure the eggs don't over-cook or else they will become dry. Place each ramekin on a plate and serve immediately. Garnish with a sprig of rosemary.

Magnolia Plantation
B&B Inn

From the 1960s through 1990, Baird Mansion served as student housing and a mecca for hippies who entered Gainesville in the 1960s. Joe and Cindy Montalto purchased the home in 1990 and painstakingly restored the building to its original grandeur. The original green and red slate roof has been preserved and much of the original floor plan of the home is still intact, including the double parlors and five bedrooms. The third floor, once the scene of dances and parties under Emmett Baird's reign, has been remodeled and now serves as the Montalto's own living space. The Montalto's have also put quite a bit of time and effort into the 1½ acres of property on which the inn sits. Extensive gardens, landscaping, and fountains have been meticulously cultivated. Charleston-style courtyards, brick walking paths, and ponds have also been added to this garden oasis.

"This is quite simply the best b&b we've ever stayed at in the States. The rooms are furnished with antique beds, claw-foot baths, and loads of other personal touches. The hosts, Cindy and Joe, are extremely friendly and Cindy's breakfasts are exquisite… The best!" —GUEST

INNKEEPERS: Joe & Cindy Montalto
ADDRESS: 309 SE 7th Street, Gainesville, Florida 32601
TELEPHONE: (352) 375-6653; (800) 201-2379
E-MAIL: info@magnoliabnb.com
WEBSITE: www.magnoliabnb.com
ROOMS: 5 Rooms; 9 Cottages; Private baths
CHILDREN: Welcome; Call ahead
PETS: Welcome; Call ahead; Resident pets

Pancetta Cheese Egg Bake

Makes 4 Servings

½ pound sliced pancetta

4 eggs

½ cup milk

1 teaspoon sugar

½ pound shredded Cheddar cheese

1 cup small curd Cottage cheese

4 tablespoons butter, softened

¼ cup flour

½ teaspoon baking powder

Preheat oven to 350°F and spray a 2-quart baking dish with non-stick cooking spray. In a small skillet, fry the pancetta until it is crisp. Drain off excess oil and cut into small pieces; set aside. In a medium bowl, beat together the eggs, milk, and sugar. Add the cheeses and butter and mix well. Stir in the flour, baking powder, and fried pancetta. Pour the mixture into the prepared dish and bake 45 minutes, or until a knife inserted in the center comes out clean.

Night Swan
Intracoastal B&B

Night Swan is perfect for guests planning small, intimate get-togethers. Looking for a romantic retreat for you and your special someone? This is it. Martha and Chuck can even help you plan your wedding, reception, rehearsal dinner, bridal luncheon, all the while providing great accommodations for your guests. They'll

help you find caterers, florists, photographers, even a notary or judge, and limo service if needed. If a romantic beach wedding is your dream, Night Swan can help you plan it.

"My fiancée and I went for a romantic engagement getaway weekend and we were very impressed. We stayed in the Dolphin Domain room and it had the most amazing view of the water! The setting was by far the most romantic I have ever seen! The staff treated us like royalty the entire stay. From the fresh baked homemade cookies in our room and making dinner reservations to the Jacuzzi tub, relaxing robes, the wonderful homemade breakfast each morning, and even the bottle of Champagne that was left in our room to help us celebrate our engagement, we would highly recommend this b&b to anyone. We plan on going back next year for our anniversary!' —GUEST

INNKEEPERS: Martha & Chuck Nighswonger
ADDRESS: 512 South Riverside Drive, New Smyrna Beach, Florida 32168
TELEPHONE: (386) 423-4940; (800) 465-4261
E-MAIL: info@nightswan.com
WEBSITE: www.nightswan.com
ROOMS: 12 Rooms; 3 Suites; Private baths
CHILDREN: Welcome
PETS: Welcome

Egg & Cheese Bake

Makes 4-6 Servings

1¼ cup egg whites, about 10-12 eggs
⅝ cup skim milk
1 teaspoon sugar
8 ounces light Monterey Jack cheese
2 ounces light cream cheese, cubed
8 ounces non-fat small curd cottage cheese
2 tablespoons margarine
¼ cup all-purpose flour
½ teaspoon baking powder

Preheat oven to 325°F. In a large bowl, beat together the eggs, milk, and sugar. Add the cheeses and margarine. Mix for 5 minutes before adding flour and baking powder. Mix well to combine. Spray an 8x8-inch baking dish with non-stick cooking spray and pour in the batter. Bake 60 minutes, or until a knife inserted in the center comes away clean. Remove from oven and allow to stand 10 minutes before serving.

Tips and Variations

You can mix this ahead of time and refrigerate it
before you are ready to bake and serve.

CASA THORN

Guests at Casa Thorn will love the great activities available in Islamorada. Kiteboarding lessons, snorkeling tours, kayak and boat rentals are all available nearby. Parasailing flights sunset cruises as well as Everglades National Park Enviro-Tours are always popular. Reefs from Key Largo to Islamorada are a diver's paradise and provide great underwater photography subjects. Guided airboat tours are also available and the Everglades Alligator Farm is a particularly interesting place to enjoy the scenery from an airboat. Not to worry, those tours are guided!

"Staying at Casa Thorn is like staying with family. The staff are caring and attentive and have great advice and tips for food and attractions on the island. They provided a list of dining options with locations and prices. They also provided beach towels and parking passes for the nearest public beach. We missed breakfast because of an early morning dive on Key Largo, but [the staff] got up early to make us bagels and fruit to take with us. The property is beautiful and spotless – the perfect island hideaway..." —GUEST

INNKEEPERS: Thorn Trainer, Cindy Dobbs, & Mary Ann Nichols

ADDRESS: 114 Palm Lane, Islamorada, Florida 33036

TELEPHONE: (305) 852-3996

E-MAIL: casathorn@webtv.net

WEBSITE: www.casathorn.com

ROOMS: 5 Rooms; Private & shared baths

CHILDREN: Children age 8 and older welcome

PETS: Small pets welcome; Resident pets

Quiche Sans Crusto

Makes 9 Servings

"We first served this Taste of Home *recipe for St. Patrick's Day
because the spinach gives it a 'green' color.
Over time, however, we have adapted the recipe
and now call it a quiche without crust. We added the bacon bits
to give the dish a great overall taste.
It's a crowd pleaser that's quick for the cook."*
—INNKEEPER, *Casa Thorn*

1 cup seasoned bread crumbs, divided
1 (9-10 ounce) package frozen chopped spinach,
     thawed and squeezed dry
3 cups 4% cottage cheese
½ cup grated Romano or Parmesan cheese
1 package bacon bits
5 eggs

Preheat oven to 350°F. Sprinkle ¼ cup of the bread crumbs into a greased 8x8-inch baking dish and bake 3-5 minutes, until golden brown. In a large bowl, combine the spinach, cottage cheese, bacon bits, cheese, 3 of the eggs, and the remaining bread crumbs. Spread the mixture over the baked crumbs. In a small bowl, beat the remaining 2 eggs and pour evenly over the casserole. Bake, uncovered, for 45 minutes, or until a knife inserted in the center comes out clean. Let stand 5-10 minutes before serving.

LA VERANDA

St. Petersburg, nicknamed the Sun-shine City, is a small town with big feel. This charming city has long been a popular tourist destination for vacation-ers from around the world. With 360 days of sunshine a year, its easy to see why.

La Veranda is situated in one of St. Petersburg's residential areas, but is still walking distance from all of the town's attractions. Visit the Salvador Dali museum, the Museum of Fine Arts, BayWalk, The Palladium, and the Pier with its aquarium, shopping, and dining. St. Petersburg is also well known for its immaculate beaches and its thriving arts community.

"Our weekend stay with Nancy was a pleasure. [La Veranda has] over ten thousand square feet of house and so many rooms to choose from, but you still feel like you're staying at your aunt's house. [It's] is also just a few minutes walk to the center of Saint Petersburg... I would definitely stay again." —GUEST

INNKEEPERS: Nancy Mayer & Jay Jones
ADDRESS: 111 5th Avenue N, St. Petersburg, Florida 33701
TELEPHONE: (727) 824-9997; (800) 484-8423
E-MAIL: info@laverandabb.com
WEBSITE: www.laverandabb.com
ROOMS: 2 Rooms; 3 Suites; Private baths
CHILDREN: Welcome
PETS: Welcome; Resident pet

La Veranda Quiche

Makes 6-8 Servings

1 stick margarine, melted
½ cup Bisquick
1½ cups half & half
½ teaspoon salt
½ teaspoon pepper
3 green onions, chopped
Filling of choice*
1 cup grated Swiss cheese
4 eggs

Preheat oven to 350°F and spray a quiche dish with non-stick cooking spray. In a medium bowl, mix together the butter, Bisquick, half & half, salt, pepper, and green onions and pour into the quiche dish. Add your favorite filling and cover with cheese. Whisk the eggs together in a small bowl and pour over the cheese. Bake 40 minutes.

Tips and Variations

*Filling suggestions: Spinach, ham, bacon, tomatoes, or zucchini. Each can be used individually or in any combination you like.

Appetizers, Soups, Salads, & Sides

Appetizers, Soups, Salads, & Sides

One of the very nicest things about life is the way we must regularly stop whatever it is we are doing and devote our attention to eating.

—Luciano Pavarotti and William Wright, *Pavarotti, My Own Story*

CHALET SUZANNE
COUNTRY INN & RESTAURANT

In the 1920s, Bertha and Carl Hinshaw, Sr. moved to Lake of the Hills, Florida. They eventually made plans with J.L Kraft, then head of the Kraft Cheese Company, to build a community complex in Florida that would offer residents golf, tennis, and other amenities. The end of the Great Depression came, however, and with it the end of the Florida land boom. Shortly thereafter, Carl passed away. Bertha, not one to sit idly by, opened Suzanne's Tavern, named after her only daughter, in 1931. The name of the inn was officially changed to Chalet Suzanne a short while later.

Bertha was determined to do for guests what she had always done for her family – make them feel at home. One week after hanging up her sign, Bertha's first guests arrived. The family loved the new inn so much that they returned every year after. Duncan Hines and his wife also stopped for a stay at Chalet Suzanne. For Christmas, the Hines family put together a list of the best places to stay in and around Florida that was sent to all of their friends and family. Eventually, the list grew to become *Adventures in Good Eating*, the first travel and leisure book in the U.S. Chalet Suzanne could be found on both the list and subsequent national publication.

INNKEEPERS: Eric & Dee Hinshaw

ADDRESS: 3800 Chalet Suzanne Drive, Lake Wales, Florida 33859

TELEPHONE: (863) 676-6011; (800) 433-6011

E-MAIL: info@chaletsuzanne.com

WEBSITE: www.chaletsuzanne.com

ROOMS: 26 Rooms; Private baths

CHILDREN: Welcome

PETS: Not allowed; Resident pets

Chalet Suzanne's Broiled Grapefruit

Makes 2 Servings

"For nearly 70 years, Broiled Grapefruit with Grilled Chicken Liver has been the featured appetizer — the first course — of Chalet Suzanne's 6-course Candlelight Dinner. The Grilled Chicken Liver was not part of the original dish, circumstances were the mother of nvention. In the 1950s, at a dinner hosted by a national food processor and attended by Clementine Paddleford, a New York Herald Tribune food editor, the Grilled Chicken Livers were not ready in time to be served as an hors d'oeuvre, but they were ready by the time the first course, Broiled Grapefruit, was to be served. At the last minute, Vita Hinshaw garnished each grapefruit serving with a grilled chicken liver and a new tradition was begun."

—Innkeeper, *Chalet Suzanne*

1 grapefruit, at room temperature
3 tablespoons butter
1 teaspoon sugar
4 tablespoons cinnamon-sugar mixture

Slice the grapefruit in half and cut the membrane around the center of the fruit. Cut around each section half, close to the membrane, so that the fruit is completely loosened from its shell. Fill the center of each half with 1½ tablespoons butter. Sprinkle ½ teaspoon of sugar over each half and then sprinkle each half with 2 tablespoons of the cinnamon-sugar mixture.

Place the grapefruit in a shallow baking pan and broil just long enough to brown the tops and heat to bubbling hot. Remove from oven and, if desired, place a cooked chicken liver (sautéed with flour, salt, and pepper) in the center of each grapefruit.

Tips and Variations

For the cinnamon-sugar mixture,
combine 1 part cinnamon with 4 parts sugar.

Don Vicente Historic Inn

Ybor City is Tampa's historic Latin quarter. Founded over 100 years ago, it is one of only two National Landmark districts in all of Florida. The Don Vicente Inn was built by Ybor City founder, Vicente Martinez-Ybor, in 1895. The building was the original planning and development office for the community. Just a few years later, the building was transformed into the El Bien Publico health care clinic. Eventually, it was renamed The Gonzalez Clinic and served the community until 1980. For the next 18 years, the

building fell into neglect. Fire and vagrants each had their way with the building, but Jack Shiver saw great potential in the historic structure. In 1998, Jack purchased the building and began painstaking and costly renovations that would last for the next two years.

In 2000, Don Vicente Historic Inn opened its doors to their first guests. This premier boutique hotel is elegantly outfitted with hardwood flooring, Persian rugs, graceful chandeliers, and period antiques collected from around the world. The inn has 16 luxurious guest rooms, two outdoor patios, a café, a front salon, and a dining room all of which can be rented out for special events.

INNKEEPER: Tessa Shiver
ADDRESS: Corner of 9th and 14th Streets, Ybor City, Florida 33605
TELEPHONE: (813) 241-4545; (800) 206-4545
E-MAIL: reservations@donvicenteinn.com
WEBSITE: www.donvicenteinn.com
ROOMS: 14 Rooms; 2 Suites; Private baths
CHILDREN: Welcome
PETS: Not allowed

Crab Cakes
with Cajun Remoulade

Makes 12-15 Servings

*"This dish is a staple at our private events.
The much asked about recipe, finally published!"*
—INNKEEPER, *Don Vicente Historic Inn*

6 slices bread
¼ cup milk
1 large egg
⅓ cup chopped onion
16 ounces crab meat,
   picked free of shells
1 cup shrimp
1 tablespoon Worcestershire sauce
1 tablespoon ground horseradish
1 teaspoon dry mustard

¼ cup mayonnaise
2 cups bread crumbs
¼ cup frying oil

Cajun Remoulade:
1 cup mayonnaise
2 tablespoons chopped onion
2 tablespoons capers
½ teaspoon
   Cajun seasoning

For the crab cakes: In a large bowl, mix together the bread, milk, and egg. Add the onion, crab, shrimp, spices, and mayonnaise and mix together to combine. Shape ⅓ cup of the mixture into a patty and roll in the bread crumbs. Repeat until all of the mixture has been formed into patties.

In a heavy-bottomed skillet over medium-high heat, heat the oil to 360°F. Fry the patties until they are golden brown, about 4 minutes, turning over if needed, and remove to a paper towel.

For the Cajun Remoulade sauce: In a small bowl, mix together all of the ingredients until just combined.

To Serve: Place the crab cakes on a serving dish and drizzle heavily with remoulade sauce.

Gram's Place

This unique inn/hostel is great for the budget minded traveler looking for a different sort of lodging experience. Each room at Gram's place has a unique musical theme. *Lonely Planet USA* had this to say, "Gram's Place is a travel experience itself." and "About as fun and funky as it gets." As this is a hostel, Gram's Place does not include breakfast as one of it's amenities, but it does, however, have two fully equipped kitchens for communal use. The inn also offers guests use of its "BYOB Bar" nicknamed Parson's Pub and overlooking the oversized Jacuzzi, sunning decks, and hammocks.

Mark Holland opened Gram's Place in 1991 after a trip to Amsterdam. Named for rocker Gram Parsons, Mark wanted a place where he could bring together people from around the world through music. The eclectic décor is a collection of rock and travel memorabilia as well as a variety of musical instruments. Afternoons at Gram's place, you'll find guests out on the porch, hanging around the bar, and enjoying impromptu jam sessions.

"A real treasure in the heart of Tampa. I was just amazed. I have never seen anything like it before. I was planning to stay at a nearby hotel, but it was full. We were even thinking of driving to Orlando when suddenly we found this place. It was just great! The atmosphere was just fantastic and very comfortable. I am planning to come back." —GUEST

INNKEEPER: Bruce Holland

ADDRESS: 3109 North Ola Avenue, Tampa, Florida 33603

TELEPHONE: (813) 221-0596

E-MAIL: gramspl@aol.com

WEBSITE: www.grams-inn-tampa.com

ROOMS: 8 Rooms; Private & shared baths

CHILDREN: Children age 5 and older welcome

PETS: Not allowed

Easy Hot Crab Dip

Makes 6-8 Servings

1 small onion
1 can crab meat, drained
1 large package cream cheese
Dill
Paprika

Preheat oven to 350°F. Finely chop the onion in a food processor. Add the cream cheese and pulse to process and combine. Add the crab meat and pulse for a few seconds. You may add dill and paprika for extra color and flavor. Place the mixture in a pie pan and bake 20-25 minutes, or until heated through. Serve with crackers.

Tips and Variations

Variation: Try using shrimp instead of crab.

ST. FRANCIS INN

The St. Francis Inn has a variety of accommodations for guests to choose from. In addition to the rooms and suites available at the main inn, guests can also stay at the inn's beach lodgings, the Creston House condominium, or Harbor 26. Each of the inn's rooms is uniquely outfitted in stylish and comfortable elegance. Breakfast is served each morning at the St. Francis main inn, and an evening social hour is a great way to get to know your fellow travelers. Guests at the St. Francis also enjoy perks around town such as free admission

to the St. Augustine Lighthouse and Museum and half-price tickets to tour the "oldest house in St. Augustine."

"The St. Francis folks set us up at Harbor 26. The place was wonderful. It was clean and comfortable with a wonderful view of the harbor below our back deck. The St. Francis folks treated us like royalty, taking us on a ghost tour, a sailboat cruise into the Atlantic, and a tour of the downtown hot spots. We really enjoyed ourselves. We went to the b&b for social hour for drinks and a wonderful tiramisu dessert. The staff was very knowledgeable and friendly. I would recommend the St. Francis Inn to anyone wanting to visit the oldest city in the United States." —GUEST

INNKEEPERS:	Joe & Margaret Finnegan
ADDRESS:	279 St. George Street, St. Augustine, Florida 32084
TELEPHONE:	(904) 824-6068; (800) 824-6062
E-MAIL:	innkeeper@stfrancisinn.com
WEBSITE:	www.stfrancisinn.com
ROOMS:	12 Rooms; 4 Suites; 1 Cottage; Private baths
CHILDREN:	Call ahead
PETS:	Small pets welcome; Call ahead; Resident pets

Chef Gary's Hot Lobster Dip

Makes 15 Servings

8 ounces cream cheese, softened

⅓ cup mayonnaise

½ cup sour cream

¾ cup Italian bread crumbs

1 cup Mozzarella cheese

1 teaspoon onion powder

½ tablespoon fresh lemon or lime juice

1 teaspoon Old Bay seasoning

¾ teaspoon Worcestershire sauce

8 ounces pasteurized lobster meat

Preheat oven to 350°F. Using a hand mixer or blender, cream together the cream cheese, mayonnaise, and sour cream. Add the bread crumbs, cheese, onion powder, citrus juice, Old Bay, and Worcestershire sauce and mix well. Fold in the lobster by hand and pour the mixture into a 2-quart baking dish. Bake 20-25 minutes, or until the top is browned and the edges are bubbly. Allow a few minutes to cool before serving with assorted crackers.

Tips and Variations

You can also use crab meat in place of the lobster for a great warm crab dip!

Seafood Dip

Makes 30 Servings

16 ounces cooked seafood –
  blue crab, shrimp, or fish, your choice
24 ounces cream cheese, softened
1 cup cocktail sauce (recipe below)
1 tablespoon chopped parsley

Using a hand mixer or a blender, combine all of the dip ingredients until smooth. Serve with assorted crackers, sliced French baguette, or toast points.

Cocktail Sauce

1 cup ketchup
1 tablespoon minced garlic
1 tablespoon hot sauce
2 teaspoons lemon juice

In a small bowl, combine all ingredients and mix well. Use in Seafood Dip above or serve with cold boiled shrimp as another great appetizer.

Strawberry Soup

Makes 4-6 Servings

"We serve this soup as part of our breakfast menu.
It also makes a great palate cleanser before an entrée."
—INNKEEPER, St. Francis Inn

2 cups sour cream
1 pound fresh strawberries
¼ cup powdered sugar
3 tablespoons honey
2 teaspoons vanilla extract

Using a food processor, blend all of the ingredients together until smooth. Garnish with fresh mint and serve cold.

Strawberries are one of Florida's biggest crops. In fact, Florida produces 15% of the total U.S. crop.

ISLAND COTTAGE OCEANFRONT VILLA INN, CAFÉ, & SPA

Island Cottage is a beachfront, island retreat like no other. Each of the inn's elegant guest rooms and suites is named for a different Caribbean destination and features romantic décor and luxurious linens. Some rooms even have a fireplace, a Jacuzzi, and/or a private balcony. A gourmet breakfast is included with your stay and home-made cookies and refreshments are available from 2-10 P.M.

A six-course dinner is available by reservation on Saturday evenings, or you can book the dining room for a private special occasion dinner for you and that special someone.

The inn also has a spa on-site for guests who need a little pampering. Treat yourself to a hot stone massage, an open-air Polynesian massage, facials, body scrubs, and aromatherapy. Other inn amenities include bikes, beach chairs, and umbrellas for guest use. The resort is also just a short ride away from some of Flagler Beach's best attractions including: river cruises, horseback riding, kayaking, sailing, and even swimming with the dolphins.

"The service was amazing, the restaurant is 5 star (seriously), and this place cannot be more adorable." —GUEST

INNKEEPERS: Toni & Mark Treworgy

ADDRESS: 2316 S. Oceanshore Blvd, Flagler Beach, Florida 32136

TELEPHONE: (386) 439-0092; (877) 662-6892

E-MAIL: tyacht@bellsouth.net

WEBSITE: www.islandcottagevillas.com

ROOMS: 4 Rooms; 5 Suites; Private baths

CHILDREN: Children age 15 and older welcome

PETS: Small dogs welcome; Call ahead

Pumpkin Corn Chowder

Makes 8 Servings

*"I wanted to create a soup for the holidays to serve in our café,
a soup unlike anything our guests could purchase anywhere else, something unique, simple to make, and delicious.
This recipe is #1 in popularity – thick, rich, and cozy!"*
—INNKEEPER, *Island Cottage Oceanfront Villa Inn, Café, & Spa*

1 (30 ounce) can pure pumpkin
2 cups salted and seasoned chicken stock,
   boiled down to ½ cup
1 quart heavy cream, or half & half
2 teaspoons ground black pepper
1 teaspoon salt, to taste
8 ounces frozen corn, thawed

Garnish:
1 teaspoon heavy cream
Fresh ground nutmeg
Fresh chives cut into 2-inch pieces

In a large, 4-quart saucepan, stir together the pumpkin, boiled
down chicken stock, cream (or half & half if you prefer), salt,
and pepper. Once mixture is fully blended, add the corn and heat
gently, stirring constantly to keep the bottom from burning. If the
soup is too thick, you can thin it with a bit of milk.

To serve: Serve the soup hot and garnish with a swirl of heavy
cream in each bowl. Sprinkle with fresh ground nutmeg and top
with 3 pieces of chive per bowl.

Night Swan
Intracoastal B&B

Night Swan is conveniently located just a short trip from any-thing and everything travelers might want or need out of a trip to New Smyrna Beach and Florida. Of course, it's also perfect for visitors in needs of some rest and relaxation, a true rejuvenating weekend taking in the sights and sounds of the ocean. From just

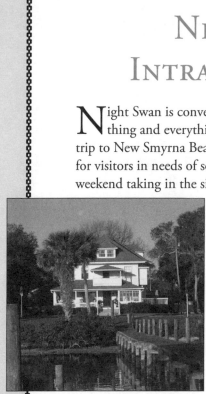

about any vantage of the inn—your room, the wrap-around porch, or the inn's own dock—you can enjoy romantic sunrises and sunsets, and watch the dolphins and the sailboats that pass in the intracoastal water-way. Leisure activities like fishing, sailing, or even romantic cruises are all available nearby.

"This place was amazing! I tagged along with my husband while he was [in town] on business and I wasn't sure what to expect at first. As soon as we got there, we were shown to our room and it was incredible. A perfect view of the lake and dock, and it was so relaxing and comforting. You can see the dolphins playing in the water all day – directly across the street! … this is the perfect place to unwind with a great book and catch up on some much needed r&r…" —GUEST

INNKEEPERS: Martha & Chuck Nighswonger
ADDRESS: 512 South Riverside Drive, New Smyrna Beach, Florida 32168
TELEPHONE: (386) 423-4940; (800) 465-4261
E-MAIL: info@nightswan.com
WEBSITE: www.nightswan.com
ROOMS: 12 Rooms; 3 Suites; Private baths
CHILDREN: Welcome
PETS: Welcome

Turkey Sausage Pinwheels

Plan ahead, these will need to freeze before cutting and baking!
Makes 6-8 Servings

2 cups Bisquick
½ cup milk
¼ cup butter or substitute
1 pound ground turkey sausage

Combine together the Bisquick mix, milk, and butter in a large bowl. Mix until blended and refrigerate 30 minutes. Divide the dough into two equal portions. Roll the first portion out on a floured surface to about ⅛-inch thickness. Spread with half of the sausage. Roll the dough lengthwise to make a long roll. Repeat with the remaining dough and sausage. Place the rolls in the freezer until they are hard enough to cut easily.

Preheat oven to 400°F. Cut the rolls into ¼-inch pieces and place on baking sheets. Bake 6 minutes before turning them over and baking an additional 6 minutes. Pinwheels should be golden brown. Serve hot and refrigerate leftovers.

Tips and Variations

Store raw pinwheels in the freezer in small batches. You can easily pull a few out and bake them up quick to go with breakfast or as snacks for when you have guests.

Broccoli Pasta Salad

Plan ahead, you will need to prepare this dish at least 3-4 hours ahead of time!
Makes 12 Servings

*"I adapted this recipe from one
that was given to my by my friend, Sam Mears."*
—INNKEEPER, *Night Swan Intracoastal B&B*

1 (10 ounce) package broccoli slaw
1 medium sweet onion, diced
2 (3 ounce) packages chicken flavored
    ramen noodles
½ cup sliced almonds
½ cup sunflower seeds

Dressing:
½ cup sugar
½ cup vinegar
½ cup oil
Flavor packets from soup

In a large bowl, toss together the broccoli slaw, diced onion, ramen noodles (raw and a bit crumbled), almonds, and sunflower seeds. In a small bowl, whisk together the dressing ingredients making sure to mix well. Pour the dressing mixture over the salad mixture and toss well to coat. Refrigerate at least 3-4 hours, or overnight, before serving.

PASTA SALAD is a popular dish that is common as easy spring and summer-time meals, especially for picnics and potlucks. They can be enjoyed hot or cold and typically are very easy to put together. Ingredients used vary widely based on the preference of the preparer but usually have one or more types of cooked pasta tossed in either a mayo-based or vinaigrette dressing. Vegetables, beans, cheese, nuts, and seafood are all popular additions.

ELIZABETH POINTE LODGE

The Elizabeth Pointe Lodge has been voted one of the best 12 waterfront inns in America and *USA Today* dubbed this unique beachside resort one of the "10 great places to sit on the porch." The inn features breathtaking ocean views and luxury accommodations that only a 3 Diamond AAA, 3 Star Mobil, and A+ FBBI rated inn can. The hardest decision you'll have to make while you're

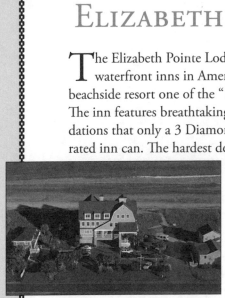

there is which room you want to stay in. Guests can choose from one of twenty guestrooms and suites in the main house, one of four larger suites in the Ocean House, or the exclusive suite in the Miller Cottage. Each room at the inn has its own unique décor and theme. Each one features decadent accommodations, though, so no matter what you choose you're guaranteed to have a vacation you'll never forget.

"From the moment this unique 'Martha's Vineyard' style inn came into view, I knew we were in for a treat… We didn't stay in the main house, but in the adjacent Ocean House (Hibiscus Room) and were awed by the décor – not cheesy beachy, but Hemingway tropical. The beach was just steps from our door and came complete with deluxe beach chairs and umbrellas. Breakfasts provided by the inn were fantastic and the wide porches were perfect for early morning coffees. The staff was gracious and accommodating. We can't wait to return!" —GUEST

INNKEEPERS: David & Susan Caples

ADDRESS: 98 South Fletcher Avenue, Amelia Island, FL 32034

TELEPHONE: (904) 277-4851; (800) 772-3359

E-MAIL: info@elizabethpointelodge.com

WEBSITE: www.elizabethpointelodge.com

ROOMS: 24 Rooms; 1 Cottage; Private baths

CHILDREN: Welcome

PETS: Not allowed

Elizabeth Pointe Lodge
Chicken Salad

Makes 10-13 Servings

*"This is our most popular menu item for ladies' lunches
such as book clubs, bridal luncheons, and the Red Hat Ladies!"*
—*INNKEEPER, Elizabeth Pointe Lodge*

9 chicken breasts
6 stalks celery, diced
2 teaspoons tarragon
$\frac{1}{8}$ teaspoon fine ground pepper
2 cups mayonnaise

The chicken breasts should be cooked in chicken broth, and then cut into bite-sized pieces (do not dice). Place the chicken, diced celery, tarragon, and pepper in a large stainless steel bowl and toss together. Add mayonnaise and toss until the chicken is moist. Place the mixture in a storage container and refrigerate until ready to be served.

We also serve this salad as a Chicken Salad Croissant Sandwich with potato chips, or as a Chicken Salad Plate — a generous portion of chicken salad served on a bed of mixed greens, garnished with seasonal fruit, and a slice of our home baked sweet bread. Both are great with a tall glass of lemonade.

Harrington House Beachfront Bed & Breakfast

Harrington House is conveniently located near some of Florida's best attractions. In nearby Sarasota and Bradenton, there are the Ringling Museum of Art, the Selby Botanical Gardens, and the Bishop Planetarium. There's also great shopping at St. Armand's Circle and four-star dining on Longboat Key. Disney World, Epcot Center, MGM, Universal Studios, and Sea World are just a two-hour drive and make a great day trip. If you're looking for something closer to the inn, try kayaking with the dolphins, take a bike tour of the island, swim and relax on the beach, or just lounge at the inn's own pool.

"My husband and I chose the Harrington House for our anniversary trip and are so glad that we did. From the fabulous view and easy beach access to the very friendly and entertaining staff, Harrington House is wonderful…. My husband and I were supposed to go on a fishing trip and we were going to miss breakfast. Knowing this, [the staff] set out bowls of cereal, bananas, and banana bread and told us that they would have milk in the fridge for us! We will definitely stay here again!" —GUEST

INNKEEPERS:	Patti & Mark Davis
ADDRESS:	5626 Gulf Drive, Holmes Beach, Florida 34217
TELEPHONE:	(940) 778-5444; (888) 828-5566
E-MAIL:	fbbi@harringtonhouse.com
WEBSITE:	www.harringtonhouse.com
ROOMS:	20 Rooms; Private baths
CHILDREN:	Children age 12 and older welcome
PETS:	Not allowed

Bombay Chicken Salad

Plan ahead, this dish needs to be prepared the day before serving!
Makes 3 Cups

"Our Bombay Chicken Salad has become very popular
with our large-party luncheon groups."

INNKEEPER, *Harrington House Beachfront B&B*

2 cups cooked chicken breast, finely diced
¼ cup golden raisins
¼ cup shredded coconut
¼ cup sliced toasted almonds
¼ cup mango chutney
¼ tablespoon curry powder
½ cup mayonnaise
Salt and pepper

Combine all ingredients in a large mixing bowl. Mix thoroughly and refrigerate for 24 hours. Serve on crackers or tea-style sandwiches (crusts removed and cut into triangles).

Tips and Variations

For extra crunch you can toast the almond slices. Preheat your oven to 350°F. Lay the nuts in a single layer over the bottom of a baking dish and bake 10-15 minutes, stirring occasionally, until nuts are golden brown. You can also toast them in an ungreased skillet over medium heat. For extra flavor, lightly toss the nuts in melted butter and sprinkle with garlic salt before toasting.

Country Sausage
& Fresh Herb Gravy

Makes 3 Quarts

*"Some mornings we use the Country Sausage & Fresh Herb Gravy
on our Eggs Benedict instead of Hollandaise Sauce.
We have a very creative and wonderful chef in our kitchen!"*
—INNKEEPER, *Harrington House Beachfront B&B*

1 ounce canola oil
1 cup finely diced white onion
12 ounces ground maple sausage
12 ounces ground sage sausage
½ cup flour
2 quarts half & half
1 tablespoon powdered chicken bouillon
½ teaspoon ground nutmeg
Salt and pepper
½ cup chopped fresh basil
½ cup chopped fresh sage
½ cup chopped fresh chives

Heat the canola oil in a 2-gallon stock-pot over medium-high heat.
Add the onion and sauté 2-3 minutes before adding the maple and
sage sausages; cook thoroughly. Lightly dust the sausage with the
flour, reduce heat to medium-low and add the half & half, chicken
bouillon, nutmeg, and salt and pepper to taste. Simmer and stir
until thickened, adding half & half as needed. Stir in the fresh herbs.
Keep the gravy over a very low heat until served.

SAUSAGE GRAVY is a popular, traditional Southern dish. The gravy is usually served over biscuits and accompanied by other breakfast fare. Some variations on biscuits and gravy include:

Egg gravy, a southern Indiana dish made by scrambling eggs in bacon grease and then adding flour, milk, and crumbled bacon.

Tomato gravy is made by mixing white gravy with crushed or diced tomatoes.

Red-eye gravy is a thin sauce made from the drippings of fried country ham that are mixed with coffee grounds. The cut side of the biscuit is then dipped in the gravy and a piece of country ham is sandwiched between the halves.

THE PENINSULA INN & SPA

In addition to its luxury guest accommodations, The Peninsula Inn & Spa is known for its critically acclaimed fine dining, and its wonderful spa. While the second and third stories of the building are given over to the guest suites and rooms, the first floor is solely devoted to the inn's other amenities.

The Seven Springs Spa is a favorite for local residents and guests alike. Here you can pamper yourself with a spa day and enjoy massages, facials, reflexology, and aromatherapy. Book a couples massage, or a girls' spa day! After all that five-star treatment and relaxation, hit the Palm Lounge and enjoy a martini or cocktail before your dinner reservation at Six Tables. Or, you can enjoy a more casual dinner of Thai-themed tapas, salads, and desserts.

Yes, there are only six tables at the inn's famous restaurant. This intimate and romantic dining experience features a candlelit six-course dinner with specialties such as the Butter Poached Shrimp, Duck Confit, and Rack of Lamb. All of the ingredients are fresh and found locally, and the menu is always changing.

INNKEEPER: Alexandra Kingzett
ADDRESS: 2937 Beach Boulevard, Gulfport, Florida 33707
TELEPHONE: (727) 346-9800; (888) 900-0466
E-MAIL: inn_spa@yahoo.com
WEBSITE: www.innspa.net
ROOMS: 11 Rooms; 5 Suites; Private baths
CHILDREN: Welcome
PETS: Welcome; Resident pet

Purée of Peas

Makes 8 Servings

"This dish is served at our restaurant,
Isabelle's Classic Southern Cuisine, which opened in 2008.
The recipe is one of my grandmother's."
—INNKEEPER, Peninsula Inn & Spa

3 (10 ounce) packages frozen peas
1 small carrot, chopped
2 scallions, halved
½ cup water
Salt and pepper, to taste
¼ teaspoon dried thyme
4 tablespoons butter
¼ cup heavy cream

Preheat oven to 300°F. Place the peas, carrots, scallions, water, salt, pepper, and thyme in a large saucepan and simmer until tender (about 8 minutes). Pour the entire mixture into a blender and process until smooth; add the butter and cream. Transfer mixture a baking dish and set the dish in a pan of hot water.
Bake 20 minutes.

HENDERSON PARK INN

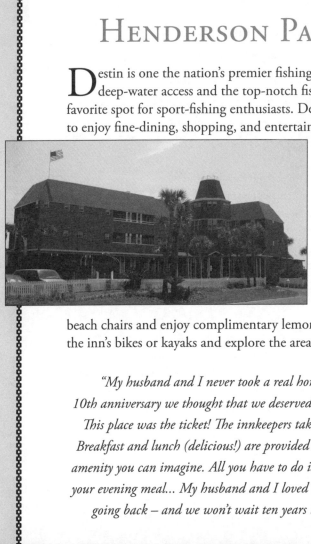

Destin is one the nation's premier fishing towns. The quick deep-water access and the top-notch fishing fleet make it a favorite spot for sport-fishing enthusiasts. Destin is also a great place to enjoy fine-dining, shopping, and entertainment. The staff at Henderson Park Inn will be glad to help you find whatever it is you are looking for whether it be a great place for dinner or a whole-day excursion. If relaxation is what you seek, soak up the rays in one of the inn's beach chairs and enjoy complimentary lemonade, or borrow one of the inn's bikes or kayaks and explore the area.

"My husband and I never took a real honeymoon so for our 10th anniversary we thought that we deserved to really spoil ourselves. This place was the ticket! The innkeepers take care of everything... Breakfast and lunch (delicious!) are provided along with every beach amenity you can imagine. All you have to do is select where you'll have your evening meal... My husband and I loved it and we'll definitely be going back – and we won't wait ten years to do so." —GUEST

INNKEEPER: **Ryan Olin**

ADDRESS: **2700 Scenic Hwy 98 E, Destin, Florida 32541**

TELEPHONE: **(850) 269-8646; (866) 398-4432**

E-MAIL: **rolin@hendersonparkinn.com**

WEBSITE: **www.hendersonparkinn.com**

ROOMS: **32 Suites; Private baths**

CHILDREN: **Cannot accommodate**

PETS: **Not allowed**

Gouda Grits

Makes 6-8 Servings

8 cups water
3 cups quick grits
2 cups heavy cream
4 cups milk
½ pound butter, cubed
3 cups Gouda cheese, grated
Salt and pepper

Lightly salt the water and bring to a boil in a large stock-pot over medium-high heat. Whisk in the grits and reduce heat to medium-low. Note that the grits will immediately return to a boil. Whisk in the heavy cream and milk and add the butter. Cook over medium-low for 30 minutes, whisking frequently. Stir in the Gouda and season with salt and pepper, to taste. Simmer to desired consistency, stirring frequently, and serve.

The term grits *can refer to any coarsely ground grain. In the U.S., however, grits commonly refers to a dish made from ground hominy.*

Pensacola Victorian B&B

A stay at the Pensacola Victorian is one full of warmth and relaxation. Breakfasts are hearty, homemade affairs that include items like Barbee's special Country Sausage Casserole, and the Spinach and Feta Quiche, all served up with fresh fruit and home-

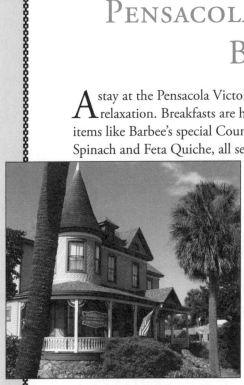

made breads. Complimentary beverages and home baked goodies are available throughout your stay. You can also enjoy a wonderful deli-style lunch at the inn's own Cottage Café where you can order quiches, salads, sandwiches, and wraps, as well as a host of home-made dessert items like Gooey Butter Cake and a variety of bread puddings (true Southern favorites!).

"If you're in the Pensacola area and want a change from the beach, then stay here! This is a charming and beautiful Victorian b&b with lovely rooms, great breakfasts, and superb hospitality; Barbee was one of the friendliest people we've ever met on our travels. Downtown Pensacola has a lot of hidden treasures so give it a whirl… you won't be disappointed." —GUEST

INNKEEPERS:	Chuck & Barbee Major
ADDRESS:	203 West Gregory Street, Pensacola, Florida 32501
TELEPHONE:	(850) 434-2818; (800) 370-8354
E-MAIL:	pcolabedbrk@pensacolavictorian.com
WEBSITE:	www.pensacolavictorian.com
ROOMS:	4 Rooms; Private baths
CHILDREN:	Welcome
PETS:	Not allowed

Country Sausage Casserole

Makes 12 Servings

"This casserole is really an adaptation of another breakfast casserole I make that uses pork sausage. As I am allergic to pork, I was never able to eat it. Eventually, I created this version so that I can eat it too! Our guests love it just as much as the original version. We serve both casseroles with our homemade waffles – it's a great combination!"

—INNKEEPER, *Pensacola Victorian B&B*

2 cups water
½ cup quick-cooking grits, uncooked
3½ cups (14 ounces) shredded Cheddar cheese
2 tablespoons extra virgin olive oil
1 tablespoon butter
1 medium onion, finely chopped
⅓ cup roasted or raw red bell pepper, finely chopped
1 (14 ounce) package Butterball smoked turkey sausage,
    finely chopped or run through a food processor to
    desired consistency
6 eggs, lightly beaten
1 cup milk
½ teaspoon black pepper
¼ teaspoon salt

Preheat oven to 350°F. Boil the water in a medium pot over medium-heat; stir in the grits and return to a boil. Reduce heat to low and cook 4 minutes, stirring occasionally. Add the cheese and stir until melted. Remove the grits from heat and set aside. Using a medium skillet over medium-high, heat the olive oil and butter. Sauté the onion and bell pepper until the onions are translucent. Add the sausage to the skillet and cook through; drain and set aside.

Using an electric mixer, blend the milk, eggs, salt, and pepper. Switch to a wooden spoon or rubber spatula and gradually stir in the grits mixture. Add the sausage mixture and stir until all of the ingredients are well blended. Pour the mixture into a lightly greased 9x13-inch baking dish or aluminum pan and bake, uncovered, for 40-50 minutes, or until the middle is set and the edges are just beginning to brown.

CASA THORN

Casa Thorn is a tropical paradise off the beaten path. Lush gardens and eclectic décor provide great character and the whole inn has an intimate charm that you'll never forget. The inn features five unique guest rooms. The Secret Garden room with its romantic Indonesian décor and private entrance give it a great secluded and romantic feel. The Moroccan Room with it's Mediterranean and African inspired décor has a hand-carved canopy bed and an elegant chandelier. Suite three has its own mini-kitchen complete with a microwave and blender. Faux animal fur rugs and tribal masks are a delightful part of this room's theme. Suite four with its red, cream, and wicker scheme has a dreamy and intimate air. The Tiki Hut shares a building with suite four. It's the best "bang for your buck" room at the inn. Guests love the affordability of this room and its charming coziness.

"We stayed in the Moroccan Room for the weekend and had a blast. [Casa Thorn] is full of interesting and quirky knick-knacks — about as far away from an anonymous hotel room as you could possibly imagine. Thorn herself is a charming hostess and is always ready with recommendations for places to eat or visit. We thoroughly enjoyed our time there and would not hesitate for a moment to go back whenever we are in the Keys." —GUEST

INNKEEPERS: Thorn Trainer, Cindy Dobbs, & Mary Ann Nichols
ADDRESS: 114 Palm Lane, Islamorada, Florida 33036
TELEPHONE: (305) 852-3996
E-MAIL: casathorn@webtv.net
WEBSITE: www.casathorn.com
ROOMS: 5 Rooms; Private & shared baths
CHILDREN: Children age 8 and older welcome
PETS: Small pets welcome; Resident pets

Ham & Cheesy Hash Brown Bake

Makes 10 Servings

"This recipe gets rave reviews whenever we serve it to our guests.
It's very filling yet doesn't weigh you down. This recipe was adapted
from Taste of Home. *We added the diced ham to the original recipe*
and reduced the number of cans of potato soup used.
It's very easy to put together and heats up in the microwave...
if there are any leftovers, that is!"

—INNKEEPER, *Casa Thorn*

> 1 (30 ounce) package frozen shredded
>   hash brown potatoes, thawed
> 1 (10¾ ounce) can condensed
>   cream of potato soup, undiluted
> 2 cups (16 ounces) sour cream
> 2 cups shredded Cheddar cheese, divided
> 1 cup grated Parmesan cheese
> 1-1½ cups diced ham

Preheat oven to 350°F. In a large bowl, combine the potatoes, soup, sour cream, 1¾ cups Cheddar cheese, all of the Parmesan cheese, and the ham. Transfer the mixture to a greased 13x9x4-inch glass baking dish. Sprinkle the remaining Cheddar cheese over the top. Bake, uncovered, 40-45 minutes, or until bubbly and cheese is melted. Let stand 5 minutes before serving.

Park Circle B&B

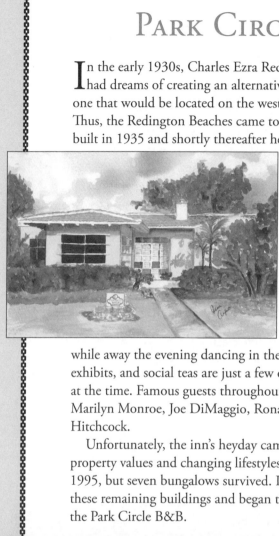

In the early 1930s, Charles Ezra Redington, a local developer, had dreams of creating an alternative to the classic Miami Beach, one that would be located on the west central coast of Florida. Thus, the Redington Beaches came to be. The very first home was built in 1935 and shortly thereafter he began a beach resort to be the social center of his grand new community. This resort, dubbed the Tides Hotel and Bath Club, opened on New Year's Eve, 1936. Soon, it became a haven for the rich and famous. Guests could rent a beach bunga-low, play cards on the patio, enjoy a meal in the finely appointed dining room, and while away the evening dancing in the ballroom. Fashion shows, art exhibits, and social teas are just a few of the events that were hosted at the time. Famous guests throughout the inn's existence include: Marilyn Monroe, Joe DiMaggio, Ronald Reagan, and even Alfred Hitchcock.

Unfortunately, the inn's heyday came to an end thanks to rising property values and changing lifestyles. The Tides was torn down in 1995, but seven bungalows survived. In 1998, the Arps family saved these remaining buildings and began their own luxury beach resort, the Park Circle B&B.

INNKEEPERS: Margaret Bourgeois & Peter Arps

ADDRESS: 16609 Gulf Boulevard, North Redington Beach, Florida 33708

TELEPHONE: (727) 394-8608; (866) 440-7275

E-MAIL: info@parkcircle.com

WEBSITE: www.parkcircle.com

ROOMS: 7 Vacation homes; Private baths

CHILDREN: Welcome

PETS: Not allowed

Italian Potato Pancakes

Makes 12 Servings

"These have a great flavor and go really well with a nice slice of ham."
—INNKEEPER, *Park Circle B&B*

1 medium onion, chopped
1 clove garlic, diced
2 pounds potatoes, shredded
1 cup shredded Parmesan cheese
¼ cup fresh basil, chopped
Salt and fresh ground pepper, to taste
Olive oil

In a large frying pan, sauté the onion and garlic until translucent. Mix the potatoes, Parmesan, basil, and salt and pepper together in a large bowl before adding the onion mixture. Pour a bit of olive oil into the heated pan (enough to cover the bottom). Scoop the entire mixture into the pan and pat down firmly. Cook 10-12 minutes over medium heat. Flip the pancake onto a large plate and slide back into the pan, uncooked-side-down. Cook an additional 10 minutes.

To serve: Slice into wedges and garnish with sour cream, tomatoes, and basil leaves.

Luncheon & Dinner Entrées

Luncheon & Dinner Entrées

> "There is no love sincerer
> than the love of food.
>
> —GEORGE BERNARD SHAW

THE MERMAID &
THE ALLIGATOR

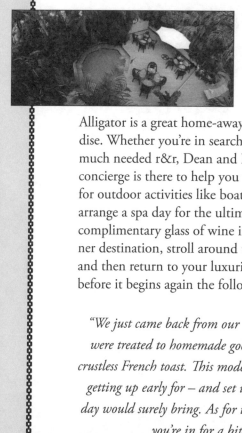

Innkeepers Dean and Paul had one goal in opening their luxury b&b in historic Key West: to create a quiet retreat from the hustle and bustle of town. In that, they have succeeded. The casual but elegant Mermaid & Alligator is a great home-away-from home in the middle of paradise. Whether you're in search of a tropical beach adventure or some much needed r&r, Dean and Paul can help. The inn's very own concierge is there to help you with dinner reservations, arranging for outdoor activities like boating, sailing, and fishing, and can even arrange a spa day for the ultimate in personal pampering. Enjoy a complimentary glass of wine in the evening as you choose your dinner destination, stroll around the town's many shops and galleries, and then return to your luxurious room for a restful night's sleep before it begins again the following day.

"We just came back from our trip to Key West.… Every morning we were treated to homemade goodies like Belgian waffles, quiche, and crustless French toast. This modest yet scrumptious meal was truly worth getting up early for – and set us straight for the many adventures the day would surely bring. As for the atmosphere… well, let's just say that you're in for a bit of paradise…" —GUEST

INNKEEPERS:	Dean Carlson & Paul Hayes
ADDRESS:	729 Truman Avenue, Key West, Florida 33040
TELEPHONE:	(305) 294-1894; (800) 773-1894
E-MAIL:	kwmermaid@aol.com
WEBSITE:	www.kwmermaid.com
ROOMS:	9 Rooms; 3 Suites; 1 Cottage; Private baths
CHILDREN:	Children age 16 and older welcome
PETS:	Not allowed; Resident pets

Sun-dried Tomato & Jalapeno Frittata

Makes 16-18 Serving

"This recipe was adapted from one found on epicurious.com."
—INNKEEPER, *The Mermaid & The Alligator*

2 (1 pound) packages extra sharp
    white Cheddar cheese
Sun-dried tomatoes
1 teaspoon diced jalapenos
6 cups liquid egg product*
1 tablespoon jalapeno juice
Chopped fresh basil
Salt and pepper

Preheat oven to 325°F. Shred the cheese in a food processor. Spray 2 quiche pans with non-stick cooking spray and pour one pound of the shredded cheese into each dish. Drain the oil from the sun-dried tomatoes and spread them evenly over the cheese. Sprinkle the diced jalapenos around and cover with the basil, salt, and pepper. In a large bowl, whip together the liquid egg and the jalapeno juice. Divide the mixture evenly between the two quiche pans.

Place the quiche pans on the center oven rack, towards the rear of the oven, and bake 35-40 minutes. The quiches will begin to brown around the edges when they are done.

Tips and Variations

If using a non-convection oven, set to 350°F and bake for 40-50 minutes.

*12-14 regular eggs plus ½ cup milk

MANGO INN

The elegant and inviting Mango Inn is a collection of three homes constructed between 1915 and 1920, the oldest of which is actually the oldest home in all of Lake Worth. These buildings were nearly lost after years of neglect and were stripped of virtually all of the original architectural elements. Extensive renovations, however, restored the homes to their present beauty and

the b&b opened doors to guests in late 1996. Today, there are a total of seven guest rooms, two suites, and one guest cottage, each with its own unique personalities. The area is quiet and seemingly secluded what with the lush tropical gardens. There's a heated swimming pool and patio area and a veranda that overlooks it all. Each morning the breakfast buffet is set up on the veranda and you can enjoy your meal in perfect serenity.

Mango Inn is situated just three blocks from Lake Worth's historic district. There you will find great antique stores, art galleries, and boutiques as well as a wide array of dining choices. There is also a large selection of museums and malls within driving distance of the inn and some of the world's best white sand beaches are just a few miles away.

INNKEEPERS: Deb & Bill Null & Judi Flynn

ADDRESS: 128 North Lakeside Drive, Lake Worth, Florida 33460

TELEPHONE: (561) 533-6900; (888) 626-4619

E-MAIL: info@mangoinn.com

WEBSITE: www.mangoinn.com

ROOMS: 7 Rooms; 2 Suites; 1 Cottage; Private baths

CHILDREN: Children age 15 and older welcome

PETS: Not allowed

Mango Inn Artichoke, Ham, & Goat Cheese Strata

Plan ahead, this dish needs to be refrigerated overnight!
Makes 8 Servings

8 large eggs
2 cups half & half
1 (6 ounce jar) marinated artichoke hearts
1 clove garlic, pressed
½ cup ham, cubed
Salt and pepper, to taste
¼ teaspoon herbes de provence*
½ teaspoon fresh chopped sage
1 cup Parmesan cheese
4 ounces goat cheese
1½ cups cubed French bread (tiny cubes)

Beat the eggs and half & half together in a large bowl. Chop the artichoke hearts and add them to the egg mixture. Stir in the garlic, cubed ham, salt and pepper, herbes to provence, sage, and Parmesan. Crumble in the goat cheese. Press the bread cubes into the mixture, cover and refrigerate overnight.

The following morning: Preheat oven to 350°F. Pour the mixture into a buttered quiche pan and bake 40-50 minutes, until the center is firm and a knife comes out clean. Cut into desired portion sizes and serve.

Tips and Variations

*Herbes de Provence is a blend of dried herbs that can be found on any spice aisle.

CAMELLIA ROSE INN

This circa 1903 Queen Anne Victorian was built for Thomas J. Swearingen, the owner of one of Gainesville's first car dealerships. The original structure had a separate kitchen for fifteen years. The home passed through some interesting hands throughout the years including George A. Dell, a grocery store owner who sold the

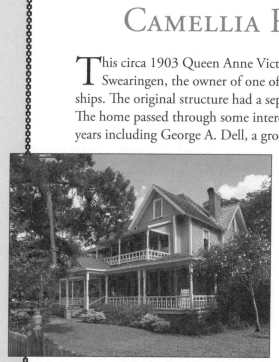

home to Hal C. Batey, who would eventually become mayor of Gainesville. Owners Pat and Tom purchased the home in 2006 and, after loving restorations, opened the Camellia Rose Inn. They've been welcoming guests with open arms ever since.

"The Camellia Rose Inn is a perfect blend of elegance and comfort. I loved every minute of my stay there. The room was peaceful, comfortable, and exceptionally clean, the innkeepers were just delightful, full of pleasant conversation and helpful information, and the breakfast was amazing! I plan to stay there every time I am in the Gainesville area." —GUEST

INNKEEPERS: Pat & Tom McCants

ADDRESS: 205 SE 7th Street, Gainesville, Florida 32601

TELEPHONE: (352) 395-7673

E-MAIL: info@camelliaroseinn.com

WEBSITE: www.camelliaroseinn.com

ROOMS: 6 Rooms; 1 Cottage; Private baths

CHILDREN: Welcome

PETS: Welcome; Call ahead; Resident pets

Tomato-Basil Quiche

Makes 6-8 Servings

1 cup shredded Cheddar cheese
1 cup shredded Monterey Jack cheese
1 cup Swiss cheese
1 tablespoon flour
6 eggs, beaten
1 tablespoon Worcestershire sauce
½ cup half & half
1 medium tomato
1 tablespoon dried sweet basil,
    or ½ cup chopped fresh basil
3-6 strips cooked bacon,
    drained and crumbled (optional)

Preheat oven to 350°F and coat an 8-inch quiche pan with non-stick spray. Combine the cheeses. In a small bowl, toss 1 cup of the cheese mixture with the flour and place in the bottom of the quiche pan. Spread the remaining cheese over the top. In a bowl, whisk together the eggs, half & half, and Worcestershire; whisk until mixture is frothy. Pour over the cheese and top with the tomato, basil, and bacon (if using). Bake 35-40 minutes, or until center is domed and nicely browned. Let stand 20-30 minutes before serving.

LAUGHING LIZARD B&B

Laughing Lizard B&B is a three story, tin-roofed, rambling cottage. This charming inn has just 4 guest rooms and a total of fifty-six windows! This means that not only does each guest receive the specialized and individual attention that they deserve, but they also enjoy breathtaking views from every angle of the inn. The atmosphere is casual and laid-back, perfect for a beach getaway, and it's adults-only. Treat yourself to a weekend with your special some-

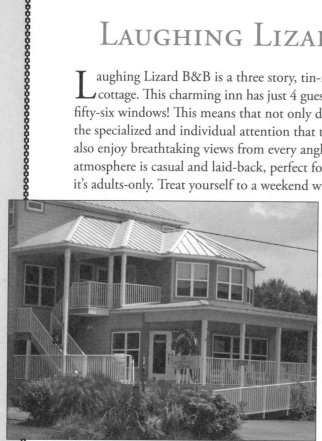

one, stay a night or stay the week, you'll never want to leave this ocean paradise.

Each of the inn's four rooms features a unique theme. From the Shy Salamander room with it's black and white décor to the Crimson Chameleon with it's bold and romantic tropical appeal, guests will love the attention to detail and the warm welcome they receive here. Walk the beach, watch the sun set, take the local trolley to beach destinations, then sip a taste of afternoon wine.

INNKEEPERS:	Bill Ockunzzi
ADDRESS:	2211 Gulf Boulevard, Indian Rocks Beach, Florida 33785
TELEPHONE:	(727) 595-7006
E-MAIL:	info@laughinglizardbandb.com
WEBSITE:	www.laughinglizardbandb.com
ROOMS:	4 Rooms; Private baths
CHILDREN:	Cannot accommodate
PETS:	Not allowed

No-Crust Spinach Quiche

Makes 6-8 Servings

1 tablespoon olive oil
1 onion, cut into small dice
1 clove garlic, finely minced
1 (10 ounce) box frozen chopped spinach,
    thawed and drained
5 large eggs, beaten
3 cups shredded Muenster cheese
¼ teaspoon salt
¼ teaspoon pepper

Preheat oven to 400°F and set your oven rack to the center position. Lightly grease or spray a 9-inch heat-resistant glass dish and set in the heating oven. Heat the olive oil in a medium skillet over medium-high heat. Add the onion and sauté, stirring occasionally, until soft. Stir in the garlic and cook until fragrant, about 1 minute. Add the spinach to the pan and continue cooking until all of the moisture has evaporated. Remove from heat.

In a large bowl, combine the eggs, cheese, salt, and pepper; stir in the spinach mixture. Carefully remove the heated glass dish from the oven and pour in the quiche mixture. Bake in oven until set, about 25 minutes. Cool slightly before slicing and serving.

PENSACOLA VICTORIAN B&B

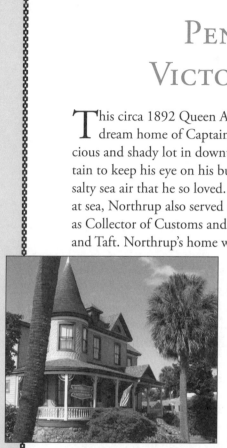

This circa 1892 Queen Anne Victorian home was once the dream home of Captain William Hazaard Northrup. The spacious and shady lot in downtown Pensacola was perfect for the captain to keep his eye on his business ventures while still smelling the salty sea air that he so loved. In addition to his distinguished career at sea, Northrup also served as Pensacola's councilman, mayor, and as Collector of Customs and Postmaster under Presidents Roosevelt and Taft. Northrup's home was a favorite gathering place for the leaders of Pensacola at the time. After his death, son Edmin moved his family into the home and continued the tradition, hosting gatherings and parties that grew to include a group of musicians and eventually led to the founding of the Pensacola Philharmonic Orchestra in 1926.

Today the home has been fully restored and still retains its historic turn-of-the-century charm. The four spacious guest rooms are beautifully appointed, the common areas are warm and welcoming, and the hosts, Chuck and Barbee, are genial and enchanting. With nearly fifty years in the hospitality industry, the Majors know how to make guests feel welcome, like they're part of the family.

INNKEEPERS: Chuck & Barbee Major
ADDRESS: 203 West Gregory Street, Pensacola, Florida 32501
TELEPHONE: (850) 434-2818; (800) 370-8354
E-MAIL: pcolabedbrk@pensacolavictorian.com
WEBSITE: www.pensacolavictorian.com
ROOMS: 4 Rooms; Private baths
CHILDREN: Welcome
PETS: Not allowed

Spinach & Feta Quiche

Makes 12 Servings

"I created this recipe as a direct result of my love for spanikopita, a Greek spinach and feta cheese pie that is baked in layers of phyllo dough. While I love eating just about anything with phyllo, I hate working with it. With this recipe, I can get all of those yummy flavors without having to wrestle with phyllo dough. We have several quiches our guests can choose from and this is the hands-down winner! We also have this quiche on our Cottage Café menu next door and it's a the best-seller there as well. Hope ya'll like it!"

—INNKEEPER, *Pensacola Victorian B&B*

3 tablespoons extra virgin olive oil
2 teaspoons chopped garlic
½ cup finely chopped onion
1 (32 ounce) package frozen
    cut leaf spinach, thawed with
    excess water squeezed out
4 ounces crumbled feta cheese
1 pie crust
10 eggs

2 cups half & half
¼ cup sour cream
½ teaspoon salt
½ teaspoon pepper
1 teaspoon Cavender's
    Greek Seasoning
8 ounces shredded Swiss cheese
⅓ cup chopped green onions
¾ cup grated Parmesan cheese

Preheat oven to 400°F and grease a 9x13-inch baking dish. Roll out the pie crust to fit your baking dish and prick the bottom. Bake until the crust is just beginning to firm up and feels slightly dry to the touch, about 10-15 minutes.

While the crust bakes, heat the oil in a large skillet over medium-high heat. Sauté the onions and garlic until the onion is translucent. Add the spinach and sauté until all ingredients are well mixed and the spinach is heated through. Remove from heat and fold in the crumbled feta. Set aside to cool. Using an electric mixer, blend together the eggs, half & half, sour cream, salt, pepper, and Greek seasoning; set aside.

When your pie crust comes out of the oven reduce heat to 350°F. Evenly spread the Swiss cheese over the crust and top with the spinach mixture. Next, carefully pour on the egg mixture. Sprinkle with green onions and Parmesan cheese and bake 1-1½ hours, or until the middle is set and edges are just beginning to brown.

River Park Inn B&B

Guests at the River Park Inn are in for a real treat. After a restful night's sleep wrapped in cozy linens, the smells of the hearty and homemade breakfast are sure to get your stomach rumbling. Mouthwatering selections include oven baked granola cereal served with bacon and fresh fruit and the inn's signature Apple Cheese Strata – layered French toast with ham, cheese, and apples.

"We went to the River Park Inn for our anniversary. We were looking for a relaxing weekend and what we found far exceeded our expectations! We were able to try several wonderful restaurants within walking  *distance of the b&b. We also took the back roads and visited several wonderful shops and antique stores. Pat and Dale are wonderful innkeepers... [and] are a wealth of information about the local area as well as nearby points of interest. The inn is beautiful and carries so much history of its own. We also enjoyed having the park and river right across the road, and having a wonderful porch to rock on and relax. We left rested and content and are already making plans for a return trip!" —GUEST*

INNKEEPERS: Pat Sickles

ADDRESS: 103 South Magnolia Avenue, Green Cove Springs, Fla. 32043

TELEPHONE: (904) 284-2994; (888) 417-0363

E-MAIL: riverparkinn@comcast.net

WEBSITE: www.riverparkinn.com

ROOMS: 5 Rooms; Private baths

CHILDREN: Children age 2 and older welcome

PETS: Not allowed; Resident pets

Spinach Cheese Bake

Makes 6-8 Servings

*"This is a nutritious crustless pie
that can be baked the night before and
warmed in the microwave the next morning
as part of a wholesome brunch."*

—INNKEEPER, *River Park Inn B&B*

2 (10 ounce) packages frozen chopped spinach
3 eggs beaten
¼ cup all-purpose flour
1 teaspoon seasoned salt
¼ teaspoon ground nutmeg
¼ teaspoon ground black pepper
2 cups creamed cottage cheese
2 cups shredded Swiss cheese

Preheat oven to 325°F. Cook the spinach per package directions; drain and set aside. In a medium bowl, combine the eggs, flour, seasoned salt, nutmeg, and pepper. Mix in the cottage cheese, Swiss cheese, and cooked spinach. Turn the mixture out into a buttered casserole dish and bake 50-60 minutes, or until a knife inserted in the center comes away clean.

Crustless Carrot Quiche

Makes 6 Servings

*"For those sleepy-heads who prefer brunch to breakfast,
this is ideal. Bake it the night before and heat it in the microwave.
It will hold well in a warmer, too."*

—INNKEEPER, *River Par Inn B&B*

2 cups finely shredded carrots
6 eggs
1¼ cups milk
1 tablespoon instant minced onion
½ teaspoon salt
¼ teaspoon ground ginger
⅛ teaspoon white pepper
1 cup shredded Cheddar cheese

Preheat oven to 350°F and butter a 9-inch quiche pan. Place the
shredded carrots in a saucepan with just enough water to cover.
Cover and simmer over medium heat until the carrots are tender,
about 5 minutes; drain thoroughly. In a large bowl, beat the eggs
with the milk, onion, salt, ginger, and pepper. Stir in the carrots
and Cheddar cheese and pour the batter into the prepared pan.
Place the filled quiche pan in a shallow pan of hot water – enough
water to come up the side of the quiche pan but not all the way
to the top. Bake 35 minutes, or until a knife inserted in the center
comes away clean. Let the quiche stand 5 minutes before serving.

QUICHES are popular breakfast items, but they also make a great lighter lunch or dinner option. The quiche, in its most basic form, is made of eggs, milk or cream, and a pastry crust. Almost any combination of meats, vegetables, and cheeses can be added to the quiche, and the crust itself can be eliminated altogether if desired.

The quiche has long been considered a classic of French cuisine, but it is quite likely that it is a German invention. The word quiche comes from the German kuchen or cake and Lorraine, of the classic Quiche Lorraine, was the eventual French name for the medieval kingdom of Lothringen, an area that was under German rule until the mid 1700s.

Quiche Lorraine, considered the original quiche, was an open pie with an egg cream custard and smoked bacon and its crust was originally made from bread dough. It was not until much later that cheese was added to the quiche. Add onions to a Lorraine and you have Quiche Alsacienne.

PALMS & ROSES B&B

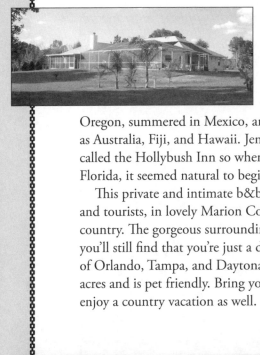

The Palms & Roses Bed & Breakfast was built in 2007 after owners Donald and Jennifer Kehl moved to Florida in 2003. The two love to travel – met and married in California, lived in Oregon, summered in Mexico, and have visited such exotic locales as Australia, Fiji, and Hawaii. Jennifer owned an inn in the UK called the Hollybush Inn so when they settled in Summerfield, Florida, it seemed natural to begin thinking about a new one.

This private and intimate b&b is located away from the crowds and tourists, in lovely Marion County – world-renowned horse country. The gorgeous surroundings are peaceful and relaxing, but you'll still find that you're just a drive away from all the attractions of Orlando, Tampa, and Daytona Beach. The inn rests on a full four acres and is pet friendly. Bring your pooch with you and let them enjoy a country vacation as well.

INNKEEPERS: Donald & Jennifer Kehl

ADDRESS: 15065 SE 73rd Avenue, Summerfield, Florida 34491

TELEPHONE: (352) 245-9022

E-MAIL: palmsandroses@gmail.com

WEBSITE: www.palmsandroses.com

ROOMS: 3 Suites; Private baths

CHILDREN: Cannot Accommodate

PETS: Welcome; Call ahead; Resident Pets

Shrimp & Cheese Quiche

Makes 4-6 Servings

6 eggs
2½ cups milk
2 tablespoons parsley, chopped
¾ teaspoon ground mustard
½ teaspoon salt
10 slices bread –
    crusts removed and cubed
2 cups salad shrimp
1 (16 ounce) block Velveeta
    cut into thin strips

Preheat oven to 325°F and grease an 11x7x2-inch baking dish. In a medium bowl, whisk together the eggs, milk, parsley, mustard and salt; set aside. Layer the cubed bread into the bottom of the baking dish. Top with the shrimp and the cheese. Pour the egg mixture over the top and bake 50-55 minutes. Allow the dish to stand 10 minutes before slicing and serving.

Spinach Meat Roll

Plan ahead, this dish needs to be refrigerated for at least one hour before baking!

Makes 4 Servings

"This dish can be prepared well in advance if you like."

—INNKEEPER, *Palms & Roses*

2 eggs, beaten
¾ cup seasoned breadcrumbs
⅓ cup ketchup
¼ cup milk
1 teaspoon salt
¼ teaspoon pepper
¼ teaspoon oregano
2 pounds ground beef
1 (10 ounce) pack frozen spinach,
    defrosted and drained
½ pound cooked ham
2 cups shredded Mozzarella cheese

In a medium bowl, beat together the eggs, breadcrumbs, ketchup, milk, ½ teaspoon salt, pepper, and oregano. Add the beef and mix well to combine. Place the mixture on a large piece of foil and pat into a 12x10-inch oblong shape. Evenly spread the spinach over the meat mixture then top with the ham and 1½ cups of cheese. Roll up the mixture and seal the seams and ends before placing seam side down on a baking sheet. Cover and refrigerate for at least 1 hour.

To bake: Preheat oven to 350°F. Bake uncovered for 1 hour and 10 minutes. Remove from oven and top with the remaining cheese.

Russian Chicken

Makes 6 Servings

"This recipe is quick and easy!"

—INNKEEPER, *Palms & Roses*

1 small bottle Russian dressing
1 packet onion soup mix
1 small jar of apricot/pineapple preserves
6 chicken breasts

Preheat oven to 325°F. In a medium bowl, mix together the Russian dressing, soup mix, and preserves. Place the chicken breasts in a 13x9-inch baking dish and pour the sauce over the top. Bake 60-70 minutes, or until chicken is done.

Russian dressing was said to have been invented in the States in the late 1800s or early 1900s. Some say the name is thanks to the fact that the recipe once contained caviar. Today, Thousand Island Dressing is sometimes used in its place although it should be noted that Thousand Island is a bit milder than actual Russian Dressing.

WICKER GUEST HOUSE

The Wicker Guest House is actually a compound of six houses that span an entire city block. The buildings form a ring around the inn's pool and tropical garden. This unique setting provides the illusion of a quiet island oasis when you're really just steps from Key West's famous Duval Street and all of its attractions. Many of the inn's twenty-one guest rooms have private porches or balconies overlooking the lush garden and cerulean pool. A complimentary continental breakfast is served each morning by the pool and the inn has barbecue pits available for guest use. There are four types of rooms to choose from: standard queen or king, large studio, deluxe, or the two bedroom suites. Each room is airy and welcom-

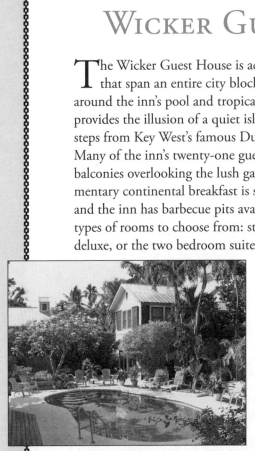

ing and may include, depending on which you choose, a kitchenette, Jacuzzi tub, and/or separate sitting area.

With an average daily temperature of 77°F, Key West is the perfect year-round vacation spot and Wicker Guest House is conveniently located in the heart of town. World-class dining, shops, boutiques, art galleries, and the-aters are all close by. The inn is also just one block from the historic Hemingway House. Snorkeling, fishing, parasailing, and sailing can all be arranged and the inn has an expert concierge on staff to help.

INNKEEPERS: Heather Whitehead

ADDRESS: 913 Duval Street, Key West, Florida 33040

TELEPHONE: (305) 296-4275; (800) 880-4275

E-MAIL: info@wickerguesthouse.com

WEBSITE: www.wickerguesthouse.com

ROOMS: 18 Rooms; 3 Suites; Private baths

CHILDREN: Welcome

PETS: Not allowed

Dad's Barbecue Chicken

Makes 4-6 Servings

"The owner, Don, loves to prepare this dish for parties
… especially employee parties!"
—INNKEEPER, *Wicker Guest House*

Barbecue sauce of choice
½ cup lemon juice
2 tablespoon garlic sauce
1 tablespoon rosemary
1 tablespoon thyme
1 chicken, whole or pieces

In a large saucepan (large enough for the chicken) mix together the barbecue sauce, lemon juice, garlic sauce, rosemary, and thyme. Cut the chicken into pieces and place in the saucepan. Bring to a boil then simmer 1½ hours.

Remove the chicken from the saucepan and place on a heated grill to finish cooking.

ISLAND'S END

Luxury and privacy are key at Island's End Resort. A private beach and ocean view are just part of what you'll experience at this peaceful oasis in St. Pete Beach, Florida. The inn is a series of guest cottages, each linked together with a wooden walkway. Each of the cottages has its own fully equipped kitchen. There are also barbecue pits and a fishing dock for guest use — you can catch and grill your own dinner! Gazebos and decks are hidden amongst lush tropical gardens and are great for guests looking to bask in the serene and sultry setting. Simply put, it's paradise.

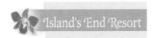

Snorkeling, deep sea fishing, art galleries, restaurants, and shopping are all in close proximity, if you're looking for something to do. The private beach is great for sunbathing, seashell hunting, and swimming. Sit on the dock and watch the dolphins or take a charter boat tour of the area. Dine in town and visit one of the night clubs, or just relax and enjoy the view. Island's End Resort and St. Pete Beach has something for everyone.

INNKEEPERS: Millard & Jona Gamble

ADDRESS: 1 Pass-A-Grill Way, St. Pete Beach, Florida 33706

TELEPHONE: (727) 360-5023

E-MAIL: jzgpag@aol.com

WEBSITE: www.islandsend.com

ROOMS: 6 Rooms; Private baths

CHILDREN: Welcome

PETS: Small dogs welcome; Call ahead; Resident pet

Smothered Chicken Breasts

Makes 12 Servings

*"This recipe was adapted from
Entertaining with The Flaming Spoons."*
—INNKEEPER, *Island's End*

5 tablespoons olive oil, divided
2 large onions, peeled sliced and
    separated into rings
8 ounces fresh mushrooms, sliced
6 boneless skinless chicken breast halves,
    flattened to ¼-inch thickness and cut in half
²⁄₃ cup all-purpose flour, divided
½ teaspoon salt
½ teaspoon ground white pepper
2 cups fat-free chicken broth
¼ cup capers, drained
½ red bell pepper, finely chopped

Heat 1 tablespoon of oil in a large non-stick skillet over medium-high heat. Add the onions and cook, stirring occasionally, until they are golden brown. Remove the onions to a bowl. Add another tablespoon of oil to the pan and sauté the mushrooms 3-5 minutes, remove and mix with the onions. Mix together ⅓ cup of the flour with the salt and pepper in a flat dish. Dip each chicken piece in the flour mixture to coat. Heat 2 tablespoons of oil in the skillet. Brown the chicken lightly on each side. Remove and arrange in one layer in a 9x13-inch baking dish; top with the onion and mushroom mixture.

Preheat oven to 375°F. Add the remaining flour and oil to the heated skillet and stir until all of the flour has been absorbed. Add the chicken broth and stir until the mixture is smooth. Cook over medium-high heat until the sauce boils and thickens to form a gravy; stir in the capers. Pour the gravy over the chicken and vegetables and bake 25 minutes, or until the chicken is cooked all the way through. Sprinkle with the chopped red bell pepper and serve.

Avera-Clarke House

The historic Avera-Clarke House is a great escape from the stresses of daily life. A scrumptious breakfast is included with every guest's stay and lunches and dinners can be arranged with prior notification.

Visitors to Monticello can enjoy bicycling, hunting, and fishing nearby. There are also a number of historic homes open for touring, and eco-tours of the area national forests and refuges. Rent a canoe or kayak and travel the nearby Wacissa, Wakulla, or St. Marks rivers, or just spend your day drinking iced tea and relaxing beneath the shade of the inn's enormous oaks and magnolias. The inn's large courtyard is also a great place to host a special event for friends and family.

INNKEEPERS: Gretchen & Troy Avera

ADDRESS: 580 West Washington Street, Monticello, Florida 32344

TELEPHONE: (850) 997-5007

E-MAIL: averaclarke@aol.com

WEBSITE: www.averaclarke.com

ROOMS: 5 Rooms; 1 Cottage; Private & shared baths

CHILDREN: Welcome

PETS: Small pets welcome; Resident pets

Sausage Pie

Makes 1 Pie

"I serve this dish with sour cream and a salad of sliced avocados, tomatoes, and onions dressed in balsamic vinaigrette. Very tasty!"
—INNKEEPER, *Avera-Clarke House B&B*

½ pound sausage
   (recommended: whole hog lean)
1 (8-inch) pie shell
3 ounces mozzarella cheese
5 eggs
¼ cups milk
Salt and pepper, to taste

Preheat oven to 325°F. Remove the sausage from the casings and brown in a non-stick skillet over medium-high heat. Remove from heat, drain, and crumble before placing sausage in the pie shell. Grate the cheese over the sausage. In a small bowl, beat together the eggs and milk; pour over the sausage and cheese. Season with salt and pepper, to taste. Bake about 40 minutes, or until the mixture is set.

Tips and Variations

You can substitute mild Cheddar or pepper Jack cheese in place of the mozzarella if you prefer.

TURTLE BEACH RESORT

Turtle Beach Resort is a luxurious tropical getaway hidden away on Siesta Key. Located on a beautiful lagoon, the inn has some of the most breathtaking views in all of Florida. The resort has a total of twenty guest rooms that vary from studios with kitchenettes and hot tubs to one-bedroom suites with king or queen beds and a hot tub on your own private patio. Bikes, canoes, kayaks, and grills

are all available for guest use and certain rooms have space for a private hammock to be set up.

The resort was originally a fishing camp and owners Gail and David are told that the shark teeth on display by the dock is actually from the Jaws movie itself. The inn is pet and kid friendly, but is also a great romantic retreat. *Frommers* voted the Turtle Beach Resort one of the "Top Ten Romantic Resorts in Florida." The inn has also gained recognition in *Conde Naste Traveler, Southern Living,* and *Coastal Living.* Watch a sunset from your private patio while sipping a glass of wine, venture out to one of the island's many beaches and watch the turtles nest (in season), or enjoy the Saturday evening drum circle. Water sports, shopping, and dining are all close by. You can even arrive by boat, the inn offers discounted docking fees for those that travel by water.

INNKEEPERS: Gail & David Rubinfeld

ADDRESS: 9049 Midnight Pass Road, Sarasota, Florida 34242

TELEPHONE: (941) 349-4554

E-MAIL: info@turtlebeachresort.com

WEBSITE: www.turtlebeachresort.com

ROOMS: 7 Rooms; 3 Suites; 10 Cottages; Private baths

CHILDREN: Welcome; Call ahead

PETS: Welcome; Call ahead

Grilled Barbecue Lamb with Rosemary

Makes 1 Leg or 8 Chops

"Easy and absolutely perfect for salad and sandwiches the next day!"

—INNKEEPER, *Turtle Beach Resort*

1 garlic clove, crushed
2 teaspoons black pepper
1 tablespoon olive oil
1 teaspoon balsamic vinegar
1 leg of lamb or 8 lamb chops
Fresh rosemary sprigs rosemary,
   stalks removed
Salt

Dressing:
1 tablespoon Dijon mustard
2 tablespoons finely chopped fresh mint
5 teaspoons fresh lemon juice
$\frac{1}{3}$ cup olive oil
Salt and pepper, to taste

In a small bowl, combine the garlic, pepper, oil, and vinegar. Rub the mixture over both sides of the lamb; cover and refrigerate 30 minutes. We recommend grilling the lamb chops 3-5 minutes per side to obtain a medium well doneness. Thicker meat will need to grill a bit longer.*

For the dressing: Combine the mustard, mint, and lemon juice. Gradually whisk in the oil to make a thick dressing. Add salt and pepper, to taste.

Tips and Variations

*The internal temperature on a medium well cut of lamb (leg or chop) will be 145°F.

Heritage Country Inn
B&B

If comfortable, quiet, and relaxing accommodations are what you seek, look no further, Heritage Country Inn has it all. This AAA 3 Diamond rated inn has seven uniquely furnished guest rooms, each with décor representing a different period in Florida's history. Each of the inn's spacious rooms comes with a wood burning fireplace, Jacuzzi tub, and handcrafted furnishings. Doors, moldings, and mantels are also hand carved using local woods to enhance the distinct décor of the rooms.

Innkeepers, Christa and Gerhard, are charming hosts who love to entertain guests. Their dedication to quality and pampering service is sure to make any stay at Heritage a memorable one. And then there's the cooking. A delectable full-course breakfast comes standard with every stay and features a gourmet selection of homemade items made from the best in seasonal fruits and vegetables. Dinner has also been added as an option at the inn. Guests can enjoy a romantic steak or fondue dinner complete with a complimentary glass of wine.

INNKEEPERS: Christa & Gerhard Gross

ADDRESS: 14343 W Hwy 40, Ocala, Florida 34481

TELEPHONE: (352) 489-0023; (888) 240-2233

E-MAIL: info@heritagecountryinn.com

WEBSITE: www.heritagecountryinn.com

ROOMS: 7 Suites; Private baths

CHILDREN: Welcome

PETS: Not allowed

Marinated Sirloin Steak on a Stone

Makes 4 Servings

"This dish originated in Germany many years ago and has found its way to the US via the inn's German owners."
—INNKEEPER, *Heritage Country Inn B&B*

8 tablespoons teriyaki sauce
8 tablespoons honey BBQ sauce
2 tablespoons garlic powder
2 tablespoons roasted garlic
2 tablespoons onion powder
$\frac{1}{8}$ teaspoon pepper
4 sirloin steaks (6-8 ounces each)
4 8x8-inch granite pieces*
4 wooden boards, for placing
    underneath granite pieces
4 pieces of cork, to fit the boards
Olive oil

Mix the first 6 ingredients in a bowl. Trim the steaks of any fat; place in a Ziploc bag and pour the marinade over them. Close the bag and marinade the steaks in the refrigerator for at least 2 hours, or up to 12 hours.

One hour before serving, place the granite stones in the cold oven. Turn the heat to 550°F and leave the stones in there for 45 minutes. Remove the steaks from the bag and wipe off excess marinade. Place the 4 boards on the counter and top each with a piece of cork. Remove the very hot stones from the oven and place one on each piece of cork. Brush the stones with a little olive oil and place one steak on each stone. The steaks will continue to cook on the stones. Flip the steaks and let everyone finish their own steak to their liking.

Serve with baked potatoes, garlic bread, and vegetables.

Tips and Variations

*You can have the granite cut for you at a granite store. Request that each piece have a groove cut around the edge, this will prevent any excess liquid from the steak from running off the stone.

Fruit Specialties, Desserts, Cookies, & Bars

Fruit Specialties, Desserts, Cookies, & Bars

Vegetables are a must on a diet.

I suggest carrot cake, zucchini bread,

and pumpkin pie.

—Jim Davis

Laughing Lizard B&B

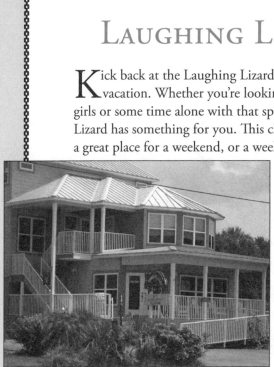

Kick back at the Laughing Lizard and treat yourself to a beach vacation. Whether you're looking for a weekend away with the girls or some time alone with that special someone, the Laughing Lizard has something for you. This charming adult's only cottage is a great place for a weekend, or a week, enjoying the sand and sun and everything else that Florida has to offer. Take a day trip to Orlando and the Disney parks, enjoy an art show or music festival, or take advantage of the award-winning golf courses. Art galleries, museums, wildlife refuges, and state parks are all within reach.

Begin your day with a mouthwatering breakfast featuring items such as the apple omelet, potato pancakes, French toast, or one of the Laughing Lizard's own fresh fruit smoothies. Spend the day lounging on the beach, or take a trip into nearby Tampa. Join your fellow guests for an evening wine-tasting before you head out to dinner, then return to your sumptuous and elegant bed before you start all over again in the morning. Laughing Lizard is definitely the kind of place you'll want to return to again and again.

INNKEEPER: Bill Ockunzzi

ADDRESS: 2211 Gulf Boulevard, Indian Rocks Beach, Florida 33785

TELEPHONE: (727) 595-7006

E-MAIL: info@laughinglizardbandb.com

WEBSITE: www.laughinglizardbandb.com

ROOMS: 4 Rooms; Private baths

CHILDREN: Cannot accommodate

PETS: Not allowed

Orange-Banana Breakfast Smoothie

Makes 1 Smoothie

"This smoothie is a great unexpected 'treat' for first time beach visitors."

—INNKEEPER, *Laughing Lizard B&B*

¾ cup orange juice
½ cup sliced banana
2 teaspoons packed brown sugar
$1/_8$ teaspoon almond extract
2 ice cubes
Fresh mint sprig, for garnish

Using a blender, combine the orange juice, banana, brown sugar, and almond extract. Add the ice cubes and blend until thick and smooth. Pour into a serving glass and garnish with a mint sprig, if desired.

Tips and Variations

For an energy kick, there's nothing like a fruit smoothie. To bump up the nutritional value, use fresh-squeezed orange juice.

ADDISON ON AMELIA

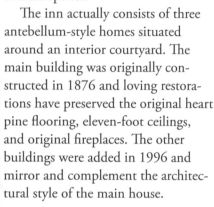

Located in Fernandina Beach's historic district is the luxurious Addison on Amelia. This tranquil fourteen-room boutique hotel is a perfect blend of elegance and history with all the modern amenities and conveniences a traveler could hope for.

The inn actually consists of three antebellum-style homes situated around an interior courtyard. The main building was originally constructed in 1876 and loving restorations have preserved the original heart pine flooring, eleven-foot ceilings, and original fireplaces. The other buildings were added in 1996 and mirror and complement the architectural style of the main house.

"… I have stayed in many b&bs, from Maine to Key West to California. The Addison on Amelia is by far the best combination of service, quality, and location that I have found. … From bicycles, beach chairs, and towels to efficient concierge service, the Addison provides anything and everything you need to ensure you have a relaxing and enjoyable time…"

—*GUEST*

INNKEEPERS: Shannon & Bob Tidball

ADDRESS: 614 Ash Street, Fernandina Beach, Florida 32034

TELEPHONE: (904) 277-1604; (800) 943-1604

E-MAIL: info@addisononamelia.com

WEBSITE: www.addisononamelia.com

ROOMS: 14 Rooms; Private baths

CHILDREN: Children age 14 and older welcome

PETS: Not allowed; Resident pet

Peach-Berry Smoothie

Make 4-5 Smoothies

"This is another guest favorite at the Addison. We love smoothies as much as we love experimenting with different fruit combinations."

—INNKEEPER, *Addison on Amelia*

1½ cups vanilla yogurt
1 cup frozen mixed berries
1 large fresh peach, peeled and pitted
About 1 teaspoon honey, to taste
1-1½ cups ice cubes

Place all of the ingredients together in a blender that can crush ice; blend until smooth. The mixture should be the consistency of a milkshake. If it's too thick, add more ice. If it's too thin, add more yogurt.

Tips and Variations

The innkeeper recommends using fat-free or light yogurt and organic fruits and honey.

Park Circle B&B

Imagine living a life of luxury and palling around with the likes of Yogi Berra, Liberace, and Marilyn Monroe. This was the Park Circle B&B years ago. Today, the seven bungalows, remains of an old resort that no longer exists, have been completely renovated with all the modern conveniences. Each is uniquely appointed and completely different from the others. Each guest house has a

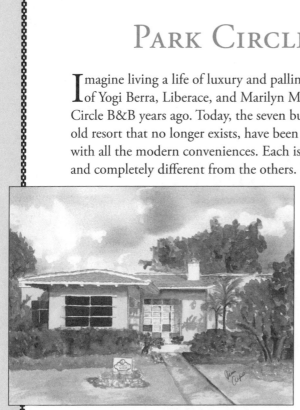

screened in porch, fully equipped kitchen, and some even have their very own garage. These bungalows encircle the inn's heated pool and are just steps from the beach.

The Manor House, where hostess Marge lives, is the central gathering place of the inn. Guests meet here for breakfast, check-in and check-out, and social gatherings like wine and cheese tastings and dessert. The owners have been in the hospitality industry for many years now, and Marge is a uniquely gifted innkeeper. She's full of information about local activities and all of the sightseeing hotspots that you won't want to miss.

INNKEEPERS: Margaret Bourgeois & Peter Arps
ADDRESS: 16609 Gulf Boulevard, North Redington Beach, FL 33708
TELEPHONE: (727) 394-8608; (866) 440-7275
E-MAIL: info@parkcircle.com
WEBSITE: www.parkcircle.com
ROOMS: 7 Vacation homes; Private baths
CHILDREN: Welcome
PETS: Not allowed

Ginger Baked Pears

Makes 4-8 Servings

"This dish is a nice surprise as a fruit serving. Our guests just love it!"
—INNKEEPER, *Park Circle B&B*

4 Anjou pears
1½ cups whipping cream
¼ cup sugar
½ teaspoon vanilla extract
¼ teaspoon ground cinnamon
Pinch of ground nutmeg
1 tablespoon fresh ginger root

Preheat oven to 375°F and lightly butter a large baking dish. Peel the pears and cut each one in half lengthwise; remove the core. Arrange each pear half, cut-side-down, in a single layer along the bottom of the baking dish. In a medium bowl, mix together the cream, sugar, vanilla, cinnamon, nutmeg, and ginger. Pour the cream mixture over the pears and bake 30-35 minutes, basting from time to time, until the pears are tender and the cream is thick and bubbly. You can serve each person a half or a whole pear. Plate in a pretty dish with a dollop of whipped cream and a slice of fresh fruit for color.

CASA THORN

This unique tropical getaway lies on Plantation Key, one of Islamorada's many islands. All of Casa Thorn is surrounded by abundant gardens and trees, making it feel like your own private paradise. Just a short walk, though, takes you right to the edge of the ocean. The inn was purchased about twenty years ago and Thorn has been transforming it into a dream vacation spot ever since.

Breakfast is served each morning on the inn's private porches. Some people never even leave their robes! The backyard pool is the ultimate in privacy and is a great place to spend the afternoon relaxing and soaking in the rays. Inside the inn, take a good look at the photos displayed around the grand piano.

Thorn and her staff love to help make your vacation as perfect as possible. They have a host of suggestions for dinner and things to do. You can walk the bike path that runs along the entire length of the Keys and get to most places you're interested in going. What could be better than that? An inn that's private and romantic, but walking distance from everything!

INNKEEPERS: Thorn Trainer, Cindy Dobbs, & Mary Ann Nichols

ADDRESS: 114 Palm Lane, Islamorada, Florida 33036

TELEPHONE: (305) 852-3996

E-MAIL: casathorn@webtv.net

WEBSITE: www.casathorn.com

ROOMS: 5 Rooms; Private & shared baths

CHILDREN: Children age 8 and older welcome

PETS: Small pets welcome; Resident pets

Baked Bananas

Makes 4 Servings

"Early in Thorn's career, she was in a television commercial that parodied the 'Chiquita Banana Girls.' We thought a banana recipe was only fitting to be served at her bed & breakfast. We tried this recipe one morning with French Toast – what a treat! You can use this dish in place of syrup. It's gooey and sweet, just right for a topping."

2 medium bananas, peeled
and cut in half lengthwise
½ cup miniature marshmallows
2 tablespoons brown sugar
1 cup corn flakes cereal
½ teaspoon ground cinnamon

Preheat oven to 375°F. Spray a small rectangular baking dish with butter-flavored non-stick cooking spray. Place the bananas in the prepared dish, cut side up. Sprinkle with marshmallows and sugar, then cover evenly with the cereal and sprinkle cinnamon over the top. Bake until the bananas are heated through and the marshmallows have melted, about 10 minutes. Serve immediately.

Tips and Variations

This recipe is great when used in place of syrup on French toast, pancakes, or waffles. You could also use it as a dessert topping over pound cake or ice cream!

THE OLD
POWDER HOUSE INN

The turn of the century Old Powder House Inn sits on a historic piece of property. The original structure, which dated back to the early 1700s, housed the gun powder used at the nearby fort. No photographs of the structure exist, but an old sketch by one Henry J. Morton suggests that by 1865, the building had been converted to an actual dwelling. This would have made it, in Morton's opinion, the oldest inhabited structure at that time.

The current home, now the Old Powder House Inn, was built in 1899 and is a great representation of the Flagler era architecture that was so popular at the time. The high ceilings, verandas, and elaborate woodwork have been preserved through the years. Ancient pecan and oak trees still remain on the property today, providing shade over the courtyard and verandas. Romance and elegance in a grand historic setting make the Old Powder House Inn the absolute best in vacation destinations. Check out the special packages on offer for that extra-special something to add to your next vacation. Champagne and chocolates, tickets to ghost tours, scenic cruises, and entry to the Colonial Spanish Quarter are all optional add-ons.

INNKEEPERS: Katie & Kal Kalieta

ADDRESS: 38 Cordova Street, St. Augustine, Florida 32084

TELEPHONE: (904) 824-4149; (800) 447-4149

E-MAIL: innkeeper@oldpowderhouse.com

WEBSITE: www.oldpowderhouse.com

ROOMS: 9 Rooms; 2 Suites; Private baths

CHILDREN: Children age 8 and older welcome

PETS: Not allowed

Katie's Breakfast Ambrosia

Plan ahead, this dish needs to refrigerate a few hours, or overnight, before serving!
Makes 8 Servings

4 large Red Delicious apples
Large bunch seedless grapes
1 (20 ounce) can pineapple tidbits,
    or half a fresh pineapple
1 (11 ounce) can Mandarin oranges,
    or 3 fresh Mandarins
1 tablespoon lemon juice
½ cup shredded coconut
½ cup walnut or pecan pieces
1 large slightly green banana
Cinnamon

Ambrosia Sauce:
¾ cup sour cream
¾ cup whipped cream, or Cool Whip
¼ cup mayonnaise
⅓ cup confectioners' sugar
1 tablespoon milk

Wash and slice the apples; remove seeds only, leave skins. Wash the grapes and halve each. Drain any canned fruit and toss in a large bowl with apple slices and halved grapes. Add lemon juice and toss again to coat. Refrigerate several hours or overnight.

To make the sauce: Add the ingredients to a medium bowl, one at a time. Mix well to combine and refrigerate several hours or overnight (this sauce can be stored in the fridge up to three days and is a great topping for any dessert).

To serve: Gently stir the coconut and nuts into the fruit mixture. Stir the ambrosia sauce and add to the fruit mixture, stirring gently to coat. Serve on dessert plates topped with a slice of banana, a sprinkle of additional nuts, and a dash of cinnamon.

Adora Inn

Located in the heart of Mount Dora's charming historic district sits the charming Adora Inn. The home was originally built in 1916 in the Arts and Crafts style popular in the latter part of the nineteenth century and early twentieth century, and was meant to be a multi-family building. Current owners, John and Arthur, fully renovated the building in 2005 paying special attention to the classic architectural details and historical aspects of the home - with a modern touch, of course. The structure itself is called the Patterson-

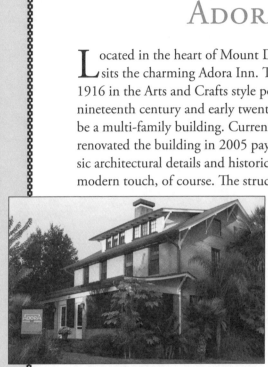

Hague House in honor of the builder and longest resident, respectively.

This three diamond AAA inn offers guests a unique and refreshing vacation experience. The innkeepers combine their extensive knowledge of the hospitality industry, cuisine, art, and design to add a truly original spin on the typical Florida boutique hotel. Each of the guest rooms features elegant décor, each one different from the others. A delectable, full course breakfast is offered daily and can be enjoyed in the elegant dining room or on the front porch. Guests may also request the inn's romantic three-course candlelight dinner or one of the Adora Inn's monthly wine tasting dinners.

INNKEEPERS:	John Cataldo & Arthur Natale
ADDRESS:	610 N. Tremain Street, Mount Dora, Florida 32757
TELEPHONE:	(352) 735-3110
E-MAIL:	info@adorainn.com
WEBSITE:	www.adorainn.com
ROOMS:	5 Rooms; 1 Suite; Private baths
CHILDREN:	Children age 8 and older welcome
PETS:	Not allowed; Resident pets

Strawberry Pizza

Makes 2 Pizzas, or 16 Servings

*"This recipe was created by Arthur's Italian grandmother
from Naples, Italy. She would make this for him
throughout his childhood. It is a classic Napolitano-style pastry
topped with fresh fruit of the season."*

—INNKEEPER *Adora Inn*

1½ cups all-purpose flour
1 stick sweet, unsalted butter,
    room temperature
¾ cup whole milk ricotta
½ teaspoon salt
Strawberries
2-3 tablespoons sugar

Preheat oven to 425°F. In a food processor fitted with a pastry
blade, blend together the flour, butter, ricotta, and salt until the
mixture forms a ball. Place dough on a floured board and divide
in half. Roll dough out to pie thickness and place each on a round
metal pizza pan. Roll the edges over and pinch to form a small
crust. Prick the dough all over with a fork. Working from the outside to the center, place thinly sliced strawberries onto the dough
in a circular pattern. Sprinkle with sugar and bake on the top rack
of the oven for 15 minutes, or until crust is golden. Slice with a
pizza cutter and serve.

PELICAN PATH B&B
BY THE SEA

O wner Tom Hubbard fondly refers to this oceanfront b&b as a "turn of the millennium bed and breakfast." Tom and Joan built the inn in 1996 after being inspired by the architecture they viewed on a trip to San Francisco. The inn opened in summer 1998 and has been welcoming guests ever since. The inn is seasonal, open from March through the end of October, perfect for enjoying Florida's wonderful summer weather.

Tom, a civil engineer, specifically designed the inn to fit on a deep and narrow lot, maximizing the space inside. Each of the four guest rooms, named for Florida birds, has a large bay window that allows for a great view of the ocean and adds additional light and space to the rooms. They each have their own unique theme and décor and private balconies or patios.

INNKEEPERS: Joan & Tom Hubbard

ADDRESS: 11 North 19th Avenue, Jacksonville, Florida 32250

TELEPHONE: (904) 249-1177; (888) 749-1177

E-MAIL: ppbandb@aol.com

WEBSITE: www.pelicanpath.com

ROOMS: 4 Rooms; Private baths

CHILDREN: Cannot accommodate

PETS: Not allowed

Pelican Path Fruit Pan Dowdy

Makes 6-8 Servings

"This recipe was given to me by my aunt 50 years ago.
She had prepared dinner, including the pan dowdy,
on the night my husband and I returned from our honeymoon.
It has been a family favorite ever since."
—INNKEEPER, *Pelican Path B&B by the Sea*

1 cup flour
1 cup sugar
2 teaspoons baking powder
1 cup milk
¾ sick butter or margarine, melted
1 can fruit of your choice,
    or fresh fruit in season

Preheat oven to 350°F. In a medium bowl, sift together the flour and baking powder. Add the sugar, milk, and melted butter and mix well to combine. Pour the batter into a greased loaf or deep dish pie pan. Pour the fruit over the top and cook for 50 minutes until lightly browned. Serve warm with whipped cream on the side.

Tips and Variations

If you are using canned fruit, drain the fruit before pouring over the batter.

River Park Inn B&B

River Park Inn B&B, in Green Cove Springs, is a great alternative to the usual St. Augustine vacation spots. Green Cove is a lovely small town full of charm and personality. Guests will appreciate the restful and relaxing atmosphere, but are still just a short drive from bustling St. Augustine. Here, you can unwind, kick back, and enjoy the slow pace this historic inn has to offer. Maps are provided for self-guided walking tours of the town, you can take a dip in the community pool, fed directly by the historic "medicinal" springs, and enjoy dining, shopping, and theaters in town. Fish or boat the St. Johns River, enjoy some great bird watching, or lounge around the inn and take in the peace and quiet.

"Relaxing, immaculate, comfortable, hospitable, historic, all these describe the wonderful accommodations [at River Park Inn]. Centrally located near the springs, restaurants, theater ... Great breakfasts, too!"
—*GUEST*

INNKEEPER: Pat Sickles

ADDRESS: 103 South Magnolia Avenue, Green Cove Springs, Fla. 32043

TELEPHONE: (904) 284-2994; (888) 417-0363

E-MAIL: riverparkinn@comcast.net

WEBSITE: www.riverparkinn.com

ROOMS: 5 Rooms; Private baths

CHILDREN: Children age 2 and older welcome

PETS: Not allowed; Resident pets

Orange Wake-Up Pie

Plan ahead, this dish needs to be prepared with time to chill before serving!
Makes 1 Pie

"This is a cool refreshing breakfast pie that is great
on a hot summer morning. The two things I like best about this recipe
are that you can bake it the night before and that you can make it
crustless if you like and save some calories. This is adapted from a
recipe that was given to me by a guest several years ago."

—*INNKEEPER, River Park Inn B&B*

2 cups cottage cheese
3 eggs
²/₃ cup sugar
2 tablespoons all-purpose flour
1 teaspoon cinnamon
1 teaspoon nutmeg
1 teaspoon grated orange rind
1 tablespoon concentrated orange juice
1 teaspoon orange extract
1 prepared pie crust, optional
1 (15 ounce) can Mandarin oranges, drained

Preheat oven to 350°F. Beat the cottage cheese with an electric mixer for 1 minute. Add the eggs, sugar, flour, cinnamon, nutmeg, orange rind, orange juice, and orange extract and blend well. Place the prepared pie crust in a 9-inch pie plate, or spray the pie plate with non-stick cooking spray if you are going crustless. Pour the batter into the pie crust or prepared pie plate and bake 50 minutes, until a knife inserted in the center comes away clean. Refrigerate overnight.

To serve: Garnish with Mandarin orange slices and serve chilled

Curry Mansion Inn

The Curry Mansion Inn sits on the historic site of William Curry's 1855 homestead. This historic Victorian mansion is still a breathtaking sight. The pillars and classic façade, the high ceilings, Tiffany glass doors, widow's walk, and veranda all speak of a more graceful past. Innkeepers, Edith and Al, purchased the home

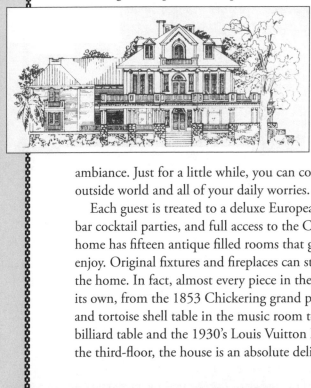

in 1974. Today, after loving restorations, the inn features 28 romantic guest rooms. Each room is elegantly appointed with wicker furnishings and period antiques. Take a step back and soak in the ambiance. Just for a little while, you can completely escape the outside world and all of your daily worries.

Each guest is treated to a deluxe European-style breakfast, open bar cocktail parties, and full access to the Curry Mansion. The home has fifteen antique filled rooms that guests can tour and enjoy. Original fixtures and fireplaces can still be seen throughout the home. In fact, almost every piece in the home has a history of its own, from the 1853 Chickering grand piano and the 1798 brass and tortoise shell table in the music room to the 1884 Brunswick billiard table and the 1930's Louis Vuitton luggage on display on the third-floor, the house is an absolute delight to see.

INNKEEPER: Edith Amsterdam

ADDRESS: 511 Caroline Street, Key West, Florida 33040

TELEPHONE: (305) 294-5349; (800) 253-3466

E-MAIL: curryinn@aol.com

WEBSITE: www.currymansion.com

ROOMS: 28 Rooms; Private baths

CHILDREN: Welcome

PETS: Small dogs welcome

Aunt Sally's Key Lime Pie

Makes 1 Pie

"Legend has it that Key Lime Pie was first invented in our kitchen!"

—*INNKEEPER, Curry Mansion Inn*

4 eggs, separated
½ cup key lime juice
1 (14 ounce) can sweetened
   condensed milk
⅓ cup sugar
Pinch cream of tartar
1 (8 inch) graham cracker crust

Preheat oven to 350°F. In a medium bowl, beat the egg yolks until they are light and thick. Blend in the lime juice and then the milk, stirring until the mixture thickens. Pour the mixture into the pie shell. In a separate medium bowl, beat the egg whites with the cream of tartar until stiff. Gradually beat in the sugar. Continue beating until glossy peaks form. Spread the egg whites over the surface of the pie, to the edge of the crust. Bake until golden brown, about 20 minutes.

Chill before serving.

THE ISLAND
HOTEL & RESTAURANT

The Island Hotel and Restaurant is one of Florida's most famous b&bs. Located in Cedar Key, this historic inn was built in 1859 using seashell tabby (shell mixed into the building material) and oak supports. The building was once a general store and a post

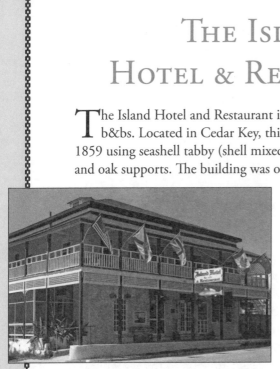

office, but surprisingly has changed very little in the almost 150 years since construction.

The restaurant at the inn first began to gain popularity in the 1940s under the watchful eye and culinary imagination of Bessie Gibbs and her cook Catherine Johnson. Bessie sold the hotel in 1973, and it wasn't until 1980 that the restaurant again began to garner praise and eventually made its way into travel guides and national (and international) magazines. Current owners, Stanley and Andy Bair, along with Chef Jahn McCumbers continue to delight guests with their attention to detail and their fabulous service. Watch a sunset from the balcony, lounge in the historic Neptune Bar, enjoy a fabulous meal, and retire in luxury. Just watch out for the ghosts. An inn with this much history, Island Hotel has 13 ghosts in residence!

INNKEEPERS: Stanley & Andy Bair
ADDRESS: 379 2nd Street, Cedar Key, Florida 32625
TELEPHONE: (352) 543-5111; (800) 432-4640
E-MAIL: islandhotel@bellsouth.net
WEBSITE: www.islandhotel-cedarkey.com
ROOMS: 10 Rooms; Private baths
CHILDREN: Welcome
PETS: Not allowed

Grannie's Carrot Cake

Makes 1 Cake

*"This recipe originally came from Marie McCain,
our current chef's grandmother. She used to make it and
add all kinds of fun stuff like coconut and pecans."*

—INNKEEPER, *The Island Hotel*

2¼ cups all-purpose flour
2 cups sugar
2 teaspoons baking soda
2 tablespoons ground cinnamon
4 eggs, beaten
1½ cups oil
3 cups shredded carrots
Cream cheese frosting

Preheat oven to 350°F. Grease and flour 3 8-inch cake pans; set aside. In a medium bowl, sift together the flour, sugar, baking soda, and cinnamon; set aside. In a large bowl, mix together the eggs and oil. Add the shredded carrots and any optional add-ins if desired. Pour the flour mixture into the carrot mixture and stir well to combine. Divide the mixture evenly between the 3 prepared pans and bake for 25-30 minutes. Cool completely before frosting and assembling. You can use with either homemade or store-bought cream cheese icing.

Tips and Variations

Variation: Add up to 1 cup of any of the following (or a combination): Ripe banana, chopped dates, coconut, pecans, crushed pineapple, or raisins.

CHALET SUZANNE®
COUNTRY INN & RESTAURANT

Since 1931, the Chalet Suzanne Inn & Restaurant has been the recipient of numerous prestigious awards including a top spot on Florida Trend Magazine's Spoon Hall of Fame. They even made it into Duncan Hines's own *Adventures in Good Eating*, one of the very first national restaurant guides. The inn offers a multi-course Prix-Fixe dinner and has recently added a la carte selections as well.

The inn features twenty-six unique guest rooms, five dining rooms, a cocktail lounge, a canning facility where the inn's famous original soups and sauces are canned – including the Moon Soup eaten by NASA's own, the courtyard spa, and the fully stocked wine dungeon. And for the most exclusive of guests, the Chalet Suzanne even has its very own 2,300 foot airstrip. Each guest at the Chalet Suzanne will love the complimentary traditional breakfast. You can also visit the wine dungeon before dinner for a bit of wine and cheese.

Four generations of Hinshaws have lived and worked at Chalet Suzanne. Though they have a full staff, the family still take part in and oversee the day-to-day operations of the inn and pride themselves on the continued success of their historic inn.

INNKEEPERS: Eric & Dee Hinshaw

ADDRESS: 3800 Chalet Suzanne Drive, Lake Wales, FL 33859

TELEPHONE: (863) 676-6011; (800) 433-6011

E-MAIL: info@chaletsuzanne.com

WEBSITE: www.chaletsuzanne.com

ROOMS: 26 Rooms; Private baths

CHILDREN: Welcome

PETS: Not allowed; Resident pets

Chalet Suzanne's Gâteau Christina

Plan ahead, this cake needs to be prepared the day before serving!
Makes 1 4-Layer Cake

*"This delicious dessert is named after
Carl & Vita Hinshaw's daughter, Christina."*
—INNKEEPER, *Chalet Suzanne*

Meringue:
4 egg whites
1½ cups sugar
⅓ cup blanched ground almonds

Chocolate Filling:
2 egg whites
½ cup sugar
2 sticks butter, softened
2 tablespoons unsweetened cocoa
4 ounces semisweet chocolate, melted

For the meringue: Preheat oven to 250°F. Cut aluminum foil into 4 8-inch circles and grease each lightly. In a medium bowl, whip the egg whites until stiff; as they begin to stiffen gradually add the sugar and almonds. Place the foil rounds on a large baking sheet and spread each evenly with meringue. Bake 15 minutes, or until the meringues are dry. Carefully turn the meringues over and bake 5 minutes longer.

For the chocolate filling: In the top of a double boiler over hot (not boiling) water, beat the egg whites until they are foamy. Gradually add the sugar, cocoa, butter, and chocolate, beating until thick and creamy. Remove from heat and cool.

To assemble the gâteau: Place the best meringue layer on the bottom and spread with chocolate. Top with another meringue, pressing down lightly to make the layers fit together, and spread with chocolate. Repeat until all of the meringues are used and the top is liberally coated with chocolate. Cover and refrigerate for at least 24 hours.

Tips and Variations

These may be stored in tin boxes for gifts.

St. Francis Inn

St. Augustine is known as the United States' oldest city. The St. Francis Inn is conveniently located just off the main drag, but steps from all that the city has to offer. Tour the historic landmarks, enjoy fine cuisine, and shop at the eclectic boutiques. Museums, art galleries, and antiques, funky clothing shops, a wax museum, and

Ripley's Believe it or Not are all right at your fingertips. Add to that the white sand beaches and the clear ocean and you've got one of the most popular vacation destinations in all of the nation.

"We just got back from a long weekend at the St. Francis Inn. It was everything I was hoping for, and more. The inn is very easy to find and is tucked back on a cobblestone side street. We were greeted warmly and told some of the history of the inn. Adele even gave us recommendations on restaurants and told us that the inn's complimentary car would be available to take us to and from dinner… The inn was so charming, with what seems to be original glass in most of the windows… We will DEFINITELY be back and would highly recommend the St. Francis to anyone seeking a quiet getaway." —Guest

INNKEEPERS: Joe & Margaret Finnegan

ADDRESS: 279 St. George Street, St. Augustine, Florida 32084

TELEPHONE: (904) 824-6068; (800) 824-6062

E-MAIL: innkeeper@stfrancisinn.com

WEBSITE: www.stfrancisinn.com

ROOMS: 12 Rooms; 4 Suites; 1 Cottage; Private baths

CHILDREN: Call ahead

PETS: Small pets welcome; Call ahead; Resident pets

Flour-less Chocolate Mousse Cake

Makes 1 Cake

7 ounces semi-sweet chocolate
1 stick butter
$^2/_3$ cup sugar, divided
6 eggs, separated
¾ cup (4 ounces) blanched
    almonds or pecans, finely chopped

Preheat oven to 325°F. Melt the chocolate in the top of a double boiler.* In a medium bowl, cream the butter and ⅓ cup sugar. Add the egg yolks and beat at high speed until the mixture is very light. Add the melted chocolate and nuts and mix well. In a separate bowl, beat the egg whites with the remaining ⅓ cup sugar until the mixture is stiff. Using a rubber spatula, fold the stiffly beaten egg whites into the chocolate batter.

Reserve ¾ cup of the batter. Pour the remaining batter into an ungreased 8-inch springform pan. Bake 30-45 minutes, or until a toothpick inserted in the center comes away clean. Allow the cake to cool before running a knife around the edge and removing the pan frame. The cake may fall some in the center, that is ok. Pour the reserved, uncooked cake batter over the top of the cake and chill well before slicing and serving.

St. Augustine Seven Layer Bars

Makes 12 Servings

"This makes a really great, gluten-free bar."

—CHEF, St. Francis Inn

7 ounces flaked coconut
1 cup butterscotch chips
6 ounces semi-sweet chocolate chips
8 ounces unsalted peanuts
1 (14 ounce) can sweetened
    condensed milk
½ cup sliced almonds

Preheat oven to 350°F and generously grease a 13x9-inch baking dish. Spread ⅔ of the coconut evenly over the bottom of the pan. Sprinkle (in layers) the butterscotch morsels, chocolate chips, and peanuts evenly over the coconut layer. Pour the sweetened condensed milk evenly over the top and sprinkle with sliced almonds and remaining coconut. Bake 20 minutes.

Allow the dish to cool completely before cutting into squares and serving.

Miss Denise's Banana Pudding

Plan ahead, this dish needs to be refrigerated before serving!
Makes 12 Servings

3 (5.1 ounce) packages instant vanilla pudding
1 (5.1 ounce) package instant banana pudding
6 cups whole milk
1 (14 ounce) can sweetened condensed milk
8 bananas
1 (16 ounce) container Cool Whip
½ cup orange juice
1 box vanilla wafers or butter cookies

Place the pudding mixes, milk, and the sweetened condensed milk in a medium mixing bowl and beat for about 5 minutes. Cover and refrigerate to set. Cut up the bananas and place them in a separate bowl with the orange juice; cover and refrigerate until the pudding has set.

To serve: Once the pudding is set, fold in the Cool Whip. Layer the cookies, pudding mixture, and bananas in a bowl and let sit for 1 hour before serving.

THE PENINSULA INN & SPA

Peninsula Inn & Spa is so much more than the usual beach inn. This historic landmark is the oldest building in Pinellas county and sits in the heart of the Gulfport art district. It's also on the Haunted Hotel Registry. The inn has a spa, cocktail lounge, and two restaurants on the premises in addition to the eleven luxury guest rooms and five guest suites.

After over two years of renovations, this inn opened its doors in late 2002. The décor is a wonderful British Colonial them with a Bali flair. Hand tooled oak furniture from Indonesia can be found in each unique and exotic guest room.

The Peninsula is also the anchor property in Gulfport's Historic Waterfront District. Art galleries, shops, and restaurants are all within easy walking distance and Gulfport Beach is just two blocks away.

INNKEEPER: Alexandra Kingzett
ADDRESS: 2937 Beach Boulevard, Gulfport, Florida 33707
TELEPHONE: (727) 346-9800; (888) 900-0466
E-MAIL: inn_spa@yahoo.com
WEBSITE: www.innspa.net
ROOMS: 11 Rooms; 5 Suites; Private baths
CHILDREN: Welcome
PETS: Welcome; Resident pet

Bourbon Custard

Makes 4-6 Servings

*"My grandmother served this at Christmas. She was a teetotaler,
but always loaded up the custard. It was always a great time!"*

—INNKEEPER, *Peninsula Inn & Spa*

1 quart milk
4 eggs, separated
1½ cups sugar
1 tablespoon flour
Bourbon

Bring the milk to a boil in a large saucepan. In a medium bowl, whisk together the egg yolks, sugar, and flour. In a small bowl, beat the egg whites and fold into the yolk mixture. Add the mixture to the milk and stir constantly – do not boil. Remove from heat and allow to cool. Add whiskey to taste and desired consistency. Top with whipped cream to serve.

Tips and Variations

Bourbon Custard also makes a great topping for bread pudding.

LA VERANDA

 Located in the heart of St. Petersburg's historic residential area, La Veranda is a great place that's away from the hustle and bustle, but still within walking distance of all the tourist attractions of St. Petersburg. It's old world charm with all the modern conveniences and amenities! The tree-lined property and the stately veranda from which the inn earned its name, are both private and romantic.

This grand abode has two guest rooms and three suites, each with its own different romantic theme. The inn also has space for corporate meetings and private events such as weddings and family reunions.

INNKEEPERS:	Nancy Mayer & Jay Jones
ADDRESS:	111 5th Avenue N, St. Petersburg, Florida 33701
TELEPHONE:	(727) 824-9997; (800) 484-8423, x8417
E-MAIL:	info@laverandabb.com
WEBSITE:	www.laverandabb.com
ROOMS:	2 Rooms; 3 Suites; Private baths
CHILDREN:	Welcome
PETS:	Welcome; Resident pet

Cinnamon Soufflé

Makes 6-8 Servings

1 loaf cinnamon raisin bread, crusts removed
1 can crushed pineapple
2 sticks margarine, melted
½ cup sugar
1 teaspoon vanilla extract
4 eggs
1 cup chopped pecans

Preheat oven to 350°F and spray a 9x13-inch pan with non-stick cooking spray. Cover the bottom of the dish with the cinnamon raisin bread and cover with the crushed pineapple, juice included. In a medium bowl, combine the butter, sugar, vanilla, and eggs. Pour the mixture over the pineapple layer and sprinkle with chopped pecans. Bake 45 minutes. Allow the dish to cool a bit before cutting into squares and serving.

INN SHEPARD'S PARK B&B

Planning a wedding? Inn Shepard's Park is a great place for small intimate events. Innkeeper, Marilyn Miller, is a registered notary and can even perform the ceremony for you. She also has experience in wedding photography and can capture those special moments you never want to forget. The inn is great for engagement parties, baby showers, birthdays, and anniversaries.

"… I don't know how anybody can stay in a chain hotel knowing that these little gems of inns are out there. [I] will definitely return with open arms. Wish I could go every weekend!" —GUEST

INNKEEPER: Marilyn Miller

ADDRESS: 601 SW Ocean Blvd, Stuart, Florida 34994

TELEPHONE: (772) 781-4244

E-MAIL: marilyn@innshepard.com

WEBSITE: www.innshepard.com

ROOMS: 4 Rooms; Private & shared baths

CHILDREN: Children age 12 and older welcome

PETS: Dogs welcome; Resident pets

Butterscotch Squares

Makes 10 Servings

½ cup butter, softened
1½ cups firmly packed brown sugar
2 teaspoons vanilla extract
2 eggs
2 cups flour
2 teaspoons baking powder
½ teaspoon salt
½ cup chopped nuts
Powdered sugar

Preheat oven to 350°F. In a medium bowl, cream together the butter and sugar; add the vanilla extract and the eggs and mix well. In a separate bowl, sift together the flour, baking powder, and salt. Add the flour mixture to the batter and mix well to thoroughly combine. Fold in the chopped nuts. Spread the mixture in a greased 9x13-inch pan and bake 25 minutes until golden brown. Remove the dish from the oven and allow to cool. Once the dish has cooled, cut into squares and dust with powdered sugar to serve.

ASH STREET INN

If a relaxing stay at the beach is what you're looking for, the Ash Street Inn is just the place for you. The inn's two historic homes enclose a central courtyard that features the inn's amazing heated swimming pool. You can sunbathe on complimentary beach towels

and chairs while enjoying fresh lemonade, tea, coffee, and homemade cookies. You may also decide to treat yourself to a massage courtesy of the inn's resident massage therapists. Relax on the inn's wraparound porch and watch the evening sunset before retiring to your room for the evening. In the morning, you'll wake to the mouthwatering smells of the Ash Street Inn's gourmet three-course breakfast. Items like the Orange French Toast, Cheesy Grits, Potato Pie, Oven Baked Cheese Omelet, and fresh biscuits are the perfect way to begin your day.

Just a short walk will take you to a number of island activities. Tour the Amelia Island Museum of History or the Kingsley Plantation. Book a sunset sailing cruise, or a horse-drawn carriage tour of the island. Fly-fishing, kayaking, wind sailing, and scuba diving are also readily available. The innkeepers at Ash Street can also help arrange a dolphin watching excursion or horseback riding along the beach.

INNKEEPERS: Jill Dorsen Chi & Samuel Chi

ADDRESS: 102 South 7th Street, Amelia Island, Florida 32034

TELEPHONE: (904) 277-6660; (800) 277-6660

E-MAIL: ashstreetinn@yahoo.com

WEBSITE: www.ashstreetinn.net

ROOMS: 10 Rooms; Private baths

CHILDREN: Children age 5 and older welcome; Call ahead

PETS: Small pets welcome; Resident pet

Oatmeal Chocolate Chip Cookies

Makes About 3 Dozen

*"Every day, as part of our afternoon, we put out lemonade
and fresh-baked chocolate chip cookies. We quickly learned
that although our guests appreciate the lemonade,
they can't seem to get enough of our cookies."*

—INNKEEPER, *Ash Street Inn*

1½ cups rolled oats	2 cups flour
2 sticks butter, softened,	1 teaspoon baking powder
but still firm	¾ teaspoon salt
¾ cup granulated sugar	12 ounces chocolate chips
¾ cup packed brown sugar	2 ounces grated
2 eggs, room temperature	semi-sweet chocolate
1 teaspoon vanilla extract	1½ cups pecans or walnuts

Preheat oven to 350°F. Place the oats in a blender or food processor
and blend until very fine; set aside. With an electric mixer, beat the
butter and sugars in a medium bowl until light, about 3 minutes.
Add the eggs one at a time and beat 20 seconds after each one is
added. Add the vanilla and beat for another 15 seconds to blend.
In a separate bowl, whisk together the flour, processed oats, baking
powder, and salt. With a large rubber spatula or wooden spoon,
blend the dry ingredients into the butter mixture. This will be
difficult as the batter will be very stiff. Add the chocolate chips,
grated chocolate, and nuts and stir until just combined.

Form the dough into 2-inch balls and place on a baking sheet covered with parchment paper. Bake on the middle rack 14-15 minutes,
or until the bottom of the cookies are browned. The cookies will
not spread much and should feel a bit soft when you take them
out, the will harden as the cool. Do not overcook them or they
will become very hard and dry when cooled.

Allow cookies to cool 2 minutes on the baking sheet before
removing to wire racks. Cool at least 30 minutes before serving.

Florida Favorites

Florida Favorites

Florida has a rich culinary history that
draws influence from all over the world.
Here we have compiled some
favorite recipes from Florida natives:
fruity cocktails, Caribbean inspired entrées,
and other dishes using Florida's
abundantly grown citrus.

Florida Orange Creamsicle

Makes 1 Drink

½ part orange juice
½ part simple syrup
1 part vodka
3 parts ice cream

Blend. Get drunk.

Key Lime Pie Cocktail

Makes 1 Drink

*This recipe is a slight variation of one found on the
Stirrings.com website. Stirrings makes a fantastic
Pie Crust Rimmer, but if you can't find it,
you can easily make your own
using graham crackers and a coffee grinder.*

1 Lime
Finely crushed graham crackers
2 parts margarita mix
1 part vanilla vodka
½ shot cream, or half & half

Run a lime wedge around the rim of a chilled martini glass. Place ¼ cup of crushed graham cracker crumbs on a flat plate or dish. Dip the martini glass in the crumbs to make a nice coating around the rim. Pour the margarita mix, vodka, and cream into a cocktail shaker with crushed ice. Shake to combine and pour into the chilled martini glass rimmed with crushed graham crackers.

Pink Flamingo

Makes 1 Drink

A light, fruity drink perfect after a long day of shopping!

2 parts Strawberry Daiquiri Mix
½ part grenadine
1½ parts rum
Crushed ice

Blend into a slushie and serve!

Jolly Mon (Extra Strength)

Makes 1 Drink

1 jigger dark rum
1 jigger coconut rum
1 jigger cream of coconut
Lime wedges
Shredded sweetened coconut, to garnish

Fill a cocktail shaker with crushed ice. Pour in the rums and cream of coconut and shake, squeeze in a bit of lime, and garnish with shredded coconut and lime wedge.

Cuban Crime of Passion

Makes 1 Drink

I'm not sure where the original version of this recipe came from, but it's the only one I've found that actually has passion fruit in it, others call for pineapple.

1½ jiggers light rum
½ jigger passion fruit nectar, or juice
1 jigger lime juice

Fill a cocktail shaker with crushed ice and pour in ingredients. Shake and strain into a chilled glass to serve.

Grapefruit Margarita

Makes 4 Drinks

This is one of my personal favorite margarita variations! Each year, my grandmother sends everyone a case of grapefruit and we have to scramble to use them all before they go bad. When they become really ripe, I juice them for drinks and baking and reserve the peels for candying.

Grapefruit wedges
Coarse Kosher salt or
   colored sugar for rimming
1 quart grapefruit juice
8-10 ounces tequila

2 ounces Grand Marnier
Simple syrup, to taste
2 limes
Mint

Run a grapefruit wedge around the edge of a margarita glass and dip the glass in either coarse salt or colored sugar for rimming, whichever you prefer (if using sugar, use less simple syrup for a better contrast between the tart grapefruit and the sugar). Pour the grapefruit juice, tequila, and Grand Marnier into a blender with ice. Blend to preferred consistency. Taste and add simple syrup and lime juice. Pulse the blender just to mix in the syrup and lime. Pour into glasses and garnish with thinly sliced mint and additional lime or grapefruit wedges.

Basil Strawberry Lemonade

Makes 1 Pitcher

Plant City, Florida is the strawberry capital of the world.

> Fresh strawberries
> Fresh basil
> Simple syrup (1 cup water plus 1 cup sugar)
> Organic lemonade

In a large jug, muddle 1-2 cups of strawberries with thinly sliced basil, to taste. To make the simple syrup, mix the water and sugar in a small saucepan over medium heat, stirring occasionally until the sugar has dissolved. Pour ⅓ cup (or to taste) hot or warm syrup over the muddled strawberries and basil. Add the lemonade and chill.

Miami Mojitos

Makes 1 Drink

*This Cuban creation has quickly gained popularity in the states. The ideal mojito is made using guarapo, a sweet sugar cane juice. If you can come by it, use it in place of the simple syrup. Another key ingredient in this drink is the mint. It's very important that you **do not** chop the mint. Place whole fresh mint leaves in your glass and muddle, or mash, them into a pulp. There is a barkeep tool called a muddler that is made especially for this. It's basically a wooden pestle that somewhat resembles a baseball bat and does double duty as a masher and a mixer. Another cool thing to try is to use an actual piece of fresh sugar cane as your muddler and then leave the piece in the glass for show.*

8-10 mint leaves	2 ounces rum
1 ounce lime juice or	Simple Syrup
3-4 lime wedges	Chilled club soda

Place the mint leaves, lime, and simple syrup into a cocktail shaker and muddle; add ice and the rum. Top off with club soda and shake. Pour into a glass and garnish with extra mint leaves and lime wedges to serve.

Sangria

Makes 1 Pitcher

6 cups Chianti wine
3 shots brandy
1 orange
1 lemon
1 lime
Cinnamon
¼-½ cup sugar, to taste
Ginger ale

Pour the wine and brandy together in a large pitcher. Squeeze half of each fruit into the pitcher and add a dash of cinnamon; stir. Fill the pitcher with ice and pour over enough ginger ale to fill. Stir and serve with thinly sliced fruit (you'll want to add the fruit just before serving, not earlier).

Hemingway Cocktail

Makes 1 Drink

1½ ounces white rum
¼ ounce maraschino liqueur*
½ ounce grapefruit juice
¾ ounce lime juice
¾ ounce simple syrup

Pour all of the ingredients into a cocktail shaker filled with ice. Shake well and strain into a chilled cocktail glass.

Tips and Variations

*Not to be confused with either maraschino cherry juice or other cherry liqueur. Maraschino liqueur is made from Marasca cherries and is less sweet than either of the others.

Santa Marta Sunrise

Plan ahead, this drink needs time to freeze!
Makes 1 Filled Pineapple

1 ripe pineapple
Dark rum
Juice from 1 lime

Chop the top off a ripe pineapple and set aside. Core the pineapple, saving as much of the flesh as possible. Cut the flesh away from the sides of the pineapple. Chop the removed flesh and return to the pineapple shell. Pour enough rum to fill about ⅔ of the shell. Replace the pineapple top and secure using large toothpicks or skewers. Place the filled pineapple in the freezer (upright so it won't spill) for 4-12 hours.

To drink: Remove your filled pineapple from the freezer. When you remove the top, the rum/pineapple mixture should be the consistency of a slushie. Squeeze lime juice over the top, stick in a straw, and enjoy!

Café Con Leche (Cuban Coffee)

Makes 1 Serving

1 cup water
Salt
1 heaping scoop dark roast coffee grounds
Milk, to taste
Sugar, optional

Heat the water and a dash of salt in a saucepan over medium-high heat. As soon as the water begins to boil, remove from heat and stir in coffee grounds; strain coffee into a mug. Whip desired amount of milk just a bit before adding to the coffee. Stir in sugar to taste. Enjoy!

Cocktail Cheese Biscuits

Makes 3 Dozen

Floridians are not afraid to party!
This recipe was submitted by one of Big Earth's own,
a native of Florida. This was one of her grandmother's favorites.
They make great finger food at parties.

1 stick butter, at room temperature,
    not butter substitute
1 cup grated sharp yellow Cheddar cheese,
    at room temperature
1 teaspoon salt
½ teaspoon cayenne pepper
1 cup flour
Pecan halves

Preheat oven to 350°F. Using a hand mixer, cream the butter in a medium sized mixing bowl. Add the cheese and blend together. Add in the salt, pepper, and flour and continue mixing until well combined. Roll the dough into small balls and press a pecan half into each to flatten. Place the slightly flattened balls onto a cookie sheet and bake 15 minutes.

Picadillo

Makes 12 servings

This popular Latin American ground beef dish is extremely versatile. Cuban and Puerto Rican varieties use Spanish olives and capers while other varieties use potatoes in the mixture. Picadillo can be used as a filling for tacos, mixed with vegetables and prepared stew-like, or served on its own with black beans and rice.

¾ cup olive oil
2 large Spanish onions
2 green bell peppers
2 garlic cloves
3 pounds ground steak
1 (2 pound) can whole tomatoes
2 tablespoons capers
1 can pitted black olives, drained
Tobasco sauce, optional

Heat the olive oil in a heavy-bottomed pot over medium-high heat. Toss in the onions, peppers, and garlic and sauté until onions are golden. Add the ground steak and cook, stirring occasionally, until the meat is no longer pink. Add the tomatoes and cook 1 hour. Add in the capers, olives, and Tabasco (to taste).

Tips and Variations

Add raisins and a splash of sherry at the end for a little sweet kick. Regular ground hamburger can be used instead of ground steak, lean is not recommended.

Cubano

Makes 4 Sandwiches

*The key to a great Cuban sandwich is the pressing.
Everyone has their own preferences as to building the sandwich,
but the pressing or grilling is always the same.*

1 loaf Cuban bread
Yellow mustard
½ pound baked ham, thinly sliced
½ pound roast pork, thinly sliced
Dill pickle slices
Swiss cheese, thinly sliced

Cut the bread in half horizontally. Spread mustard on both the top and bottom halves of the bread and layer with ham, pork, pickles, and Swiss cheese. Cover and cut into sandwiches.

To press: Grill the sandwiches using a buttered sandwich press or Foreman grill. The sandwich is done when it is flat, the bread is browned, and the cheese is nice and melted. You may also use a griddle if you don't have a sandwich press. Simply place the sandwich on the griddle and flatten with a heavy iron skillet or even a foil-covered brick.

Orange Margarita Shrimp

Makes 4 Servings

2 ounces tequila
Zest of 1 lime
2 tablespoons lime juice
2 tablespoons olive oil
1 tablespoon honey
Pepper
1 pound small shrimp, peeled and cleaned
1 orange, peeled and sectioned
½ tablespoon orange juice
2 large red onions
2 tablespoons freshly chopped cilantro

Place the tequila, lime zest, lime juice, oil, honey, and pepper in a Ziploc bag and shake to mix. Add in your raw shrimp and allow to marinate 10-20 minutes. Pour the shrimp and marinade into a hot skillet over medium-high heat and cook until the shrimp are pink (3-4 minutes). Remove the shrimp using a slotted spoon and bring the marinade to a boil. Reduce to about ⅓ cup, stir in the orange pieces and the orange juice, and heat through.

To serve: Thinly slice the red onions and lay them in a layer on a serving plate. Top with the cooked shrimp and then pour over the heated marinade. Season to taste and top with chopped cilantro and additional lime wedges.

Tips and Variations

This would be great with just about any combination of citrus fruit and juice. Try using grapefruit in place of the orange pieces and juice.

Key Lime Pie

Makes 2 Pies

This is a recipe you rarely see outside the home!
I love it! It's creamy and ohh so good!

1 pound 3 ounces cream cheese
2 (14 ounce) cans sweetened condensed milk
1 cup key lime juice, or fresh lime juice
2 graham cracker pie shells

Place the cream cheese, condensed milk, and lime juice in a blender (do not hand mix) and blend at high speed for 5 minutes. Pour the batter into the pie shells and chill until firm. Serve with whipped cream topping.

Tips and Variations

You can also make this as individual Key Lime Pie Tarts, use prebaked mini-tart shells and spoon a bit of the pie batter into each. Chill as above.

Sour Orange Pie

Makes 1 Pie

Sour orange trees were the native trees in Florida and provided root stock for grafting the sweeter varieties and making the sweeter Valencias more cold hearty. The juice is great for marinating pork or chicken as well as fish and shrimp. Bottles of the juice can be found in Cuban/Hispanic stores. You want it fresh? Come to Florida!

25 ginger snaps, crushed
½ stick butter, melted
4 egg yolks, beaten
2 can sweetened condensed milk
6-8 ounces sour orange juice

Preheat oven to 325°F. Mix together the crushed ginger snaps and the butter and press into a 9-inch pie plate to make a crust. Bake until nicely browned but still moist (pie shell works great for any pie or pudding).

While the pie crust bakes, mix together the egg yolks, condensed milk, and orange juice. Pour the mixture into the top of a double boiler over medium heat and cook until thickened. At this point, you can pour the mixture into the crust and chill, or you can make a meringue with the reserved egg whites. Serve with whipped cream if you are not topping with meringue.

For the meringue: Beat the reserved egg whites until frothy. Gradually add 8 tablespoons of sugar and 1 teaspoon of vanilla extract. Continue beating until stiff peaks form. Spoon over the pie and bake in preheated oven (preheated from baking your crust) 15-18 minutes, until peaks are slightly browned.

Candied Grapefruit Peel

Makes 10 Servings

These make a great snack.
You can also chop them and use them in baking
in place of candied orange peel or even candied ginger
for an interesting variation on a favorite baked item.

Rinds from 5 grapefruit
Water
4 teaspoons salt, divided
4 cups sugar

Cut the grapefruit rinds into strips of desired size. Place the rind strips in a saucepan over medium-high heat. Cover with water and add 2 teaspoons of salt. Boil 3-4 minutes. Drain and repeat. Boil twice in plain water. Drain and add 3 cups sugar to the pot. Lower heat and cook, stirring often, until moisture is gone. Remove from heat and allow to cool until you can handle the rinds with your hands. Place the last cup of sugar on a flat surface and roll the rinds in the sugar to coat. Lay on way paper to dry.

Store these in a tightly covered container. If they get sticky, allow them to air dry on wax paper again.

Florida Grapefruit Biscuits

Makes 1 Dozen

*Another great way to use up Florida grown grapefruit!
This recipe comes from an old Florida church cookbook,*
Lake Hamilton's Treasure of Personal Recipes *(1956).
It also appeared in a 2002* Food & Wine Magazine *article.*

3 cups all-purpose flour
1 tablespoon baking powder
1 teaspoon salt
½ teaspoon baking soda
6 tablespoons cold butter
1 tablespoon sugar
1 teaspoon grated grapefruit zest
1 cup grapefruit juice
Milk, for brushing
Sugar in the raw, for sprinkling

Preheat oven to 425°F. In a large bowl, sift together the flour, baking powder, salt, and baking soda. Cut the butter into the mixture and crumble together until it has a coarse, sandy texture. In a small bowl, rub the sugar into the grapefruit zest until the sugar is a deep pink color. Add the grapefruit juice and stir until the sugar has dissolved. Pour the juice mixture into the flour mixture and stir together just until the dough forms – do not over mix. Scrape the dough out onto a floured surface and knead 2-3 times. Roll the dough out to ½-inch thickness and cut using a 2-inch biscuit cutter. Place the biscuits on a cookie sheet and lightly brush the tops with milk. Sprinkle with sugar if desired. Bake 15 minutes, or until they have risen and are slightly browned on the bottom. Allow to cool before serving.

Geographical List of Inns

Alphabetical List of Inns

Recipe Index

The Bed & Breakfast Cookbook Series

New England Bed & Breakfast Cookbook
(CT, MA, ME, NH, RI, & VT)
$19.95 / 320 pages / ISBN 978-1-889593-12-8

North Carolina Bed & Breakfast Cookbook
$19.95 / 320 pages / ISBN 978-1-889593-08-1

Pennsylvania Bed & Breakfast Cookbook
$19.95 / 304 pages / ISBN 978-1-889593-18-0

Virginia Bed & Breakfast Cookbook
$19.95 / 320 pages / ISBN 978-1-889593-14-2

Washington State Bed & Breakfast Cookbook
$19.95 / 320 pages / ISBN 978-1-889593-05-0

Texas Bed & Breakfast Cookbook revised and updated
$19.95 / 304 pages / ISBN 978-1-889593-20-3

California Bed & Breakfast revised and updated
$19.95 / 312 pages / ISBN 978-1-889593-21-0

Georgia Bed & Breakfast Cookbook
$21.95 / 296 pages / ISBN 978-1-889593-19-7

Florida Bed & Breakfast Cookbook
$21.95 / 292 pages / ISBN 978-1-889593-22-7

Also Available from 3D Press

Southern Church Suppers
$19.95 / 306 pages / ISBN 978-1-889593-16-6

High Altitude Baking
$14.95 / 192 pages / ISBN 978-1-889593-15-9

3D Press, a division of Big Earth Publishing
1637 Pearl Street • Suite 201 • Boulder, CO 80302

TO ORDER, CALL: (800) 258-5830 or (303) 541-1506 or Fax: (303) 443-9687
or visit our website at www.bigearthpublishing.com